Unlocking

YOUR TRUE POTENTIAL

Harnessing Control for a Blissful
Mind, Body, and Spirit

JESSICA MARTIN

Copyright

© MMXXIII Jessica Martin/Rabbit's Pantry LLC dba Journeying with Jessica

All Rights Reserved

Limits of Liability/Disclaimer of Warranty

The author and publisher of this book and the accompanying materials have used their best efforts to prepare this program. The author and publisher make no representation or warranties with respect to the accuracy, applicability, fitness, or completeness of the contents of this program. They disclaim any warranties (expressed or implied), merchantability, or fitness for any particular purpose.

The author and publisher shall in no event be held liable for any loss or other damages, including but not limited to special, incidental, consequential, or other damages. As always, the advice of a competent legal, tax, accounting, medical or other professional should be sought. The author and publisher do not warrant the performance, effectiveness, or applicability of any references listed in this book. All links are for informational purposes only and are not warranted for content, accuracy or any other implied or explicit purpose.

This book contains material protected under International and Federal Copyright Laws and Treaties. Any unauthorized reprint or use of this material is prohibited.

I dedicate this book to my husband, Mike. He has stood by my side and sometimes dragged me along to reach my potential. The journey started from his unwavering love.

ACKNOWLEDGEMENTS

Joy, you always take my calls, no matter the time and day. Your encouragement and passion for helping the world inspire and drive all those around you to be and do more. You constantly tell me to do more, and you've sparked this into reality. You planted a seed I couldn't help but love and foster. Thank you!

I had a book inside me. Turns out I had several. With Jim Edwards pushing me along, this is possible. Thank you!

CONTENTS

Introduction 1

Chapter 1 3

Unlocking Happiness: The Key Factors Holding You Back From Achieving A Healthier Body, Happier Mind, And Growing Spirit

Chapter 2 21

The Intertwined Journey: Exploring The Connection Between Physical Health And Spiritual Growth

Chapter 3 47

The Transformation Begins: Simple Yet Powerful Practices For Spiritual Growth

Chapter 4 69

Finding Your Inner Drive: Uncovering Motivation For Personal Growth

Chapter 5 85

Embrace Your Beautiful Self: Cultivating Self-Love And Compassion Towards Oneself

Chapter 6 102

Setting Boundaries: Your Guide To Establishing Healthy Relationships And Protecting Your Well-Being

Chapter 7 117

Breaking Chains, Embracing Freedom: Overcoming Destructive Habits For Personal Progress

Chapter 8 134

Rediscovering Your True Path: Guidance For Reconnecting With Your Purpose In Life

Chapter 9 153

The Path To A Healthier And Happier Life: Setting Achievable Goals And Creating Your Action Plan

Chapter 10 170

Spiritual Practices In A Busy World: Incorporating Sacred Rituals Into Daily Life

Conclusion 187

Meet The Author 190

INTRODUCTION

Congratulations on taking the first step towards rediscovering your true potential! As you hold this book in your hands, know that you have already embarked on a journey that will help you regain control over your health, happiness, and spiritual growth.

In *"Unlocking Your True Potential: Harnessing Control for a Blissful Body, Mind, and Soul,"* I have incorporated what worked for me and works for thousands of clients and students. As a certified yoga and meditation teacher, astrologer, coach, speaker, healer, and herbologist, I aim to provide you with practical advice, tips, and examples to master this critical aspect of your life.

Finding yourself in a situation where you feel hopeless and struggling is something many of us have experienced. However, it's important to remember that you have the power to transform your life. This book is designed specifically for individuals like you who are focused on getting happy again and are determined to create a healthy body, happy mind, and growing spirit without resorting to pills or gimmicks. Instead, it offers the truth and guidance you must start your journey towards a fulfilling and vibrant life.

Why should you trust this book?

First and foremost, my credentials speak for themselves. Throughout my life, I have dedicated myself as a lifelong student to various spiritual practices and healing modalities, allowing me to gather a wealth of knowledge and experience. With decades of experience and thousands of clients healed, I have witnessed firsthand the transformative power of the principles and techniques I share in this book.

Let's dive into the book and see what awaits you.

Chapter 1

Unlocking Happiness: The Key Factors Holding You Back from Achieving a Healthier Body, Happier Mind, and Growing Spirit

"Your beliefs become your thoughts, your thoughts become your words, your words become your actions, your actions become your habits, your habits become your values, and your values become your destiny."

— **Mahatma Gandhi**

- Discover the key factors contributing to feeling stuck and hopeless, and unlock the path to a healthier body, happier mind, and growing spirit.
- Break free from societal pressure and expectations that lead to a sense of hopelessness and being trapped in an undesirable situation.
- Overcome doubt and lack of self-belief to achieve your desires and remove the mental barriers holding you back.
- Surround yourself with positive, supportive relationships to maintain a hopeful mindset and outlook on life.

- Find clarity and direction in your life to escape the feeling of aimlessness and create a sense of purpose that leads to fulfillment.

Like most of us, we desire happier, fuller lives. Feeling stuck and hopeless can hinder our progress and sense of fulfillment. Grasping the key contributors to these feelings is crucial in finding hope and breaking free from the perceived prison of society.

Girl, hold my water...I'm stepping on the soap box for a hot minute now. Let's address the elephant in the room for these feelings – It is societal pressure and expectations. When I speak of "society," this is in the context of what we are told, taught, and exposed to as we grow in life. This is from our families, friends, social circles, media, and the structure of society. Society often sets unrealistic standards for physical appearance, success, and happiness. We do this through comparing. We compare ourselves to our siblings, friends, and anyone else out there. We are going to dig into this later. But realize that when we compare ourselves to these societal ideals and fall short, well, it can lead to a sense of hopelessness and being stuck in an undesirable situation.

How's your "lack" of self-belief and confidence? That's another area we need to be aware of. When we doubt our abilities to achieve our desires, it can create a mental barrier that makes progression seem impossible. This lack of belief in ourselves can limit our potential, leading to feeling trapped in our current circumstances.

Now, look at your support system/structure. Even positive relationships can contribute to our feelings. The people we surround ourselves with significantly impact our mindset and outlook on life. There is a reason they say "circle of influence"; these people influence the way we see our worlds and ourselves. If we are surrounded by negativity and judgment, or feel unsupported, it can be challenging to find hope and maintain a positive mindset.

Heck, many parts of this complicated game of life bring us to challenges, and we find we don't have clarity and direction in life. Haven't we all been here? Wondering what we are doing, who we are, and what's our purpose? I know I'm not the only one who went through this. It's one of my highest-attended classes. When we don't have clear desires or a sense of purpose, we may feel like we are wandering aimlessly without a sense of fulfillment. This lack of direction can make it blinding to see a way out of our current situation and hinder our ability to find hope.

Oh my God, don't forget about our baggage. Like for reals, who can open their own luggage store? Raise your hand. The presence of our past, be it memories, past relationships, or unresolved emotional issues, can weigh heavily on us and make it challenging to experience a healthier body, happier mind, and growing spirit. Girl, we are digging this up too! No matter how big or small, this is there, always playing in the conscious when triggered and the subconscious mind. These unresolved issues can manifest as a sense of hopelessness and feeling stuck, as they continue to influence negative thought patterns and behaviors.

So, now that I've ripped the band-aid off, and you see we are diving into your things...keep reading! I'm a full skyline of sunshine here. We must act and combat these feelings of being stuck and hopeless. It is important to take specific steps towards finding hope and breaking free from society's prison. Redefining success and happiness based on personal values and priorities, rather than societal norms, can create a healthier mindset and a increased positive outlook on life, building self-belief, confidence, and resilience through personal development practices, such as your patterns and messaging programmed into you. All these practices can help us overcome this vicious circle and bring in the full happiness that we never knew could exist.

I'm going to date myself here. But for those of you who remember this commercial, you will get it. Got a buddy... "My buddy and me."... Who are you hanging out with? Who do you let in your sphere? Are they positive, supportive, and like-minded? We can create a stable environment, fostering hope and growth just by the energies of awesome peeps. Setting a clear vision and developing a sense of purpose provides you with a sense of direction and motivation to overcome obstacles and whatever else life projects on you.

When we dig deep, like real deep, trusting the journey, we hold the key to unlocking our potential. We find hope, break free from the prison of society, create our abundant lives, and ultimately experience a healthier body, happier mind, and growing spirit. Remember, it is the attention to detail, awareness, and deliberate approach that will cultivate a sense of stability and bring about your transformation.

Don't worry. I'm here the whole time. I got you. This is where we start.

To assist you in this journey, I hooked you up with a checklist that provides specific steps and strategies to cultivate a healthier mindset and promote personal growth. Follow this checklist and pay attention to the details. You can create stability and experience your desired transformation of a healthier body, happier mind, and growing spirit.

Checklist

1. **Identify societal pressure and expectations:** Recognize how unrealistic standards set by society contribute to feeling stuck, empty, alone, and hopeless.

2. **Build self-belief and confidence:** Work on overcoming self-doubt and cultivating a positive mindset through personal development practices like affirmations, gratitude, and self-care.

3. **Cultivate positive relationships:** Surround yourself with like-minded and supportive people who contribute to your growth and well-being.

4. **Set clear targets and develop a sense of purpose:** Define what success and happiness mean to you based on personal values and priorities. Create a roadmap to achieve them.

5. **Address past experiences and unresolved emotions:** Seek professional help or guidance to address these.

6. **Take proactive actions towards personal growth and development:** Be intentional and deliberate in your efforts to grow, learn, and overcome obstacles.

7. **Increase your awareness:** Focus on the smaller aspects of your life and patterns that need improvement and take steps to address them along the way.

8. **Seek stability:** Cultivate a sense of stability in your life by investing time and effort in creating a solid foundation for your well-being.

9. **Embrace transformation:** Be open to change and accept the process of personal transformation, understanding that it takes time and effort.

10. **Maintain perseverance:** Stay determined and committed to your journey, even when faced with setbacks or challenges.

After considering this comprehensive list, let's look at some examples I've seen so you can find meaning in this, looking at how each step can be applied in real-life situations. These examples share the importance of identifying societal pressures, building self-belief, cultivating positive relationships, setting clear desires, addressing past experiences, actively pursuing personal growth, having awareness, seeking stability, embracing transformation, and maintaining perseverance to overcome obstacles and achieve personal success and happiness!

Phew, that was a mouthful…

Let's talk about Sally. Sally was constantly bombarded with images of people who had it all together and who didn't look like her on social media. She felt pressured to conform to these unrealistic standards and believed she would never be truly happy or confident until she looked like them. This led her to feel stuck and hopeless, as she believed she could not escape the judgment and expectations of society.

Joanne wanted to start her own business, but she constantly doubted her abilities and fears of failure. She believed she would never be successful and that her dreams were out of reach. This lack of self-belief created a mental barrier, making it difficult for Joanne to take the necessary steps towards her desires, leaving her feeling stuck and hopeless.

Looking at Mary, she struggled with her circle of influence (friends and family), who constantly brought her down and made negative comments about her aspirations and dreams. Negativity and lack of support make it hard for us to stay motivated and positive about our future. She started to feel trapped in her current circumstances and unsure if she could ever find a way out.

Lacking clarity on direction, Toni had a job that paid well and provided stability, but she felt unfulfilled and lost. She didn't have a clear sense of purpose or any desires beyond her current job. This lack of direction made it challenging for Toni to see a way out of her unfulfilling situation, leading to a feeling of being stuck and alone.

Past experiences can be like a bottomless pit that many don't even realize they are stuck in. Jennifer experienced an event in her childhood that she never properly addressed or resolved. These unresolved emotions continued to haunt her, leading to feelings of hopelessness and a sense of being trapped. She believed she would never be able to move forward and find true happiness and fulfillment.

Can you see it? How societal pressure, lack of self-belief, unsupportive relationships, lack of clarity and direction, and unresolved past experiences can contribute to your life?

We can and will break free from these negative emotions. Finding hope, fulfillment, and powerful purpose.

Here is how it works in a real scenario. Let's dive into all the things.

Case Study: Finding Hope and Breaking Free from Society's Prison

Sarah, a 28-year-old woman, was struggling with feelings of being stuck and hopeless in her life. She felt trapped by societal expectations and pressures, lacked self-belief and confidence, and did not have a supportive network of relationships. Sarah also lacked clarity and direction in life, having unresolved emotional issues from past experiences.

She desperately wanted change and a better life experience. She showed up! Getting to work and sticking to it, Sarah attended coaching sessions to help her redefine success and happiness based on her own values and priorities. She learned to focus on her personal growth and well-being rather than comparing herself to societal standards.

She then realized she must incorporate daily practices of positive affirmations, gratitude exercises, and self-care routines to build her self-belief and confidence. She started writing down affirmations, acknowledging her accomplishments, and prioritizing self-care activities like meditation and exercise.

Healthy relationships were lacking. Sarah evaluated her relationships and identified unsupportive ones. She actively sought out like-minded people and joined a community that aligned with her desires and values. She formed strong, positive relationships that provided support, encouragement, and a sense of belonging.

By default, Sarah started working with a life coach to set clear, achievable desires and develop a sense of purpose. She identified her passions and what brings her joy, which allowed her to create a vision for her future. Setting specific milestones and creating action plans helped her gain direction and motivation.

Throughout the journey, she continued to practice awareness to address her past experiences. Through therapy, she learned coping mechanisms and processing techniques and gained a better understanding of how her unresolved emotional issues were impacting her current situation.

Sarah put in the work! And she achieved so much.

Improving her mental well-being, Sarah experienced a noticeable improvement. She reported feeling more optimistic, confident, and motivated in her daily life. She had a clearer vision of her desires and a stronger sense of purpose.

Sara's self-belief and confidence levels significantly increased. She no longer doubted her abilities and recognized her strengths and accomplishments. This newfound confidence allowed her to take risks and break free from her comfort zone.

Adjusting relationships isn't easy, and it takes time. However, Sarah showed up and successfully cultivated a network of supportive relationships. She developed strong bonds with people who shared her values and provided encouragement and support. This positive network boosted her morale and contributed to her overall sense of well-being.

By setting clear desires and developing a sense of purpose, Sarah gained clarity and direction in her life. She had a roadmap for her personal growth and knew the steps required to achieve her desired outcomes.

It wasn't all rainbows and sunshine. It took time! She hit walls and had ample choices to make.

Sarah faced challenges in overcoming negative thought patterns that were deeply ingrained due to past experiences. It required consistent effort, therapy, coaching, and self-reflection to challenge and change these thought patterns.

Initially, Sarah struggled to find like-minded people who shared her values and desires. It took time and persistence to connect with supportive people and establish meaningful relationships.

Not only did she push through, but she also gained lifelong lessons to help herself in the future.

Learning her comparison of herself to societal standards was detrimental to her progress and well-being. She understood the importance of defining her own version of success and happiness.

Sarah discovered the significance of prioritizing self-care. Taking care of her physical, mental, and emotional well-being helped her build resilience and maintain a positive outlook. This, she said, was the secret to her perseverance. Starting the day with her first.

Through the implementation of specific actions and initiatives, Sarah successfully found hope and broke free from society's prison. She achieved measurable outcomes in terms of improved mental well-being, increased self-belief and confidence, a supportive network, and clarity of purpose. Sarah overcame challenges, learned valuable lessons, and experienced a transformative journey towards a healthier body, happier mind, and growing spirit. Finding hope became the catalyst for her personal growth and overall well-being.

This has given you a lot to process. Reviewing the examples and Sarah's transformative journey, let's look at some mistakes to avoid when pursuing a path towards unlocking your potential. These mistakes can hinder progress and impact your ability to find hope and create a fulfilling life.

Don't slow down. Sometimes, during these exercises, you are going to hit speed bumps, roadblocks, or a brick wall. Don't give up. It's normal to have this happen. You must keep showing up and keep digging deeper, becoming more aware and sticking to what you can control and change. Little by little, you will get there. Some days, you will have massive breakthroughs, and you will feel as light as a feather and so full of happiness. Other days, you might find yourself thinking about your journey and experiences in deep digging with me, processing to figure out how this all feels, looks, and shows up for you. Allow the flow in full awareness.

Let's wrap up because I have your first digging project!

We just covered:

- **Breaking free from societal pressure:** Redefining success and happiness based on your own values and priorities, not society's unrealistic standards.
- **Believing in ourselves:** Building self-belief, confidence, and resilience through affirmations, gratitude, and self-care.

- **Staying positive:** Seeking out supportive and like-minded people who will uplift and encourage you on your journey.
- **Finding your purpose:** Setting clear desires and developing a sense of purpose to provide motivation and direction in your life.
- **Healing and letting go:** Addressing past experiences and unresolved emotions to release the weight that's holding you back and unlocking a healthier body, happier mind, and growing spirit.

Now, get digging!

In all the exercises, you need to take your time. Find a place where you won't be disturbed. Get comfortable and say to yourself this is your time, and you are doing it to grow. This is the most important time in your life. Truly think on the question and answer in your own words. No one else is going to read this. They aren't going to correct your spelling or check for readability. It's simple journaling with prompts. Just let the words flow.

Putting pen to paper opens an area of our brain that allows us to process differently. It is important to use the worksheets to gain your full experience and breakthroughs.

Here is a quick exercise to help you with these questions. Bear with me, just try it, it works!

Read the question and process it. If the answer doesn't come to you right away, no worries. Sit comfortably and close your eyes. Slow your breathing by taking a deep breath and releasing it out of your mouth. Allow your body to sink in.

As you sit here (breathing uncontrolled natural breaths), ask yourself the question in your head. Don't control the brain's thoughts. Just allow whatever flows in. Don't dismiss a memory or experience. These are crumbs leading you to the cookie jar.

The first few times, this might take a hot minute. It's cool. As you practice, you will be more efficient in identifying these thoughts and experiences.

After a moment, if you can't think of the answer to the question, or you are finding yourself frustrated, you have a choice. Either come back to it later when you don't have responsibilities popping into your thought patterns, or simply ask your creator, guide, or whatever you believe in to show you the answer.

1. What led me to feel stuck and hopeless?

_____
_____
_____
_____

2. What mental barrier is holding me back and making this seem impossible?

_____
_____
_____
_____

3. Am I surrounding myself with the right people?

_____
_____
_____
_____

4. Do I have a clear direction?

_____
_____
_____
_____

5. Which areas of my life do I feel like I can get quick, successful wins out of to improve my current state?

_____
_____
_____
_____

6. What can build my self-belief, confidence, and resilience?

_____
_____
_____
_____

7. Do I need to make changes to my environment to foster hope and growth?

_____
_____
_____
_____

8. What can provide a sense of direction and motivation to overcome obstacles when I hit them?

_____
_____
_____
_____

9. Am I ready for a massive transformation? Why am I ready now?

_____
_____
_____
_____

Phew, that was heavy huh? You can put the shovel down; we are done digging for today. Next, we are going to visit the connection between physical health and spiritual growth. Keep reading to discover how taking care of your body can have a profound impact on nurturing your spirit and leading a truly fulfilling life.

Chapter 2

The Intertwined Journey: Exploring the Connection between Physical Health and Spiritual Growth

"Your body is a temple, but only if you treat it as one."

- Astrid Alauda

- Unlock the secrets to spiritual growth by prioritizing your physical health.
- Discover the power of a healthy body in enhancing awareness, meditation, and self-reflection.
- Experience the profound connection between physical and mental well-being on your spiritual journey.
- Boost your discipline, commitment, and dedication through a focus on physical well-being.
- Learn how neglecting your physical health can hinder your spiritual growth and overall well-being.

The connection between physical health, mental health, and spiritual growth is a topic of great importance and significance. It's dear to my heart and what changed my world. It is undeniable that a strong correlation exists between these three, as they are integral aspects of our overall well-being. By nurturing and prioritizing our physical health, we lay a solid foundation for positive mental health and spiritual growth. I see so many chronically ill people with this very disconnect. It just happens with the pressures of society we give way to. It sucks us in like a magnetic pull, and before we know it, we are lost.

Here is some interesting information for you to think about. Where do you believe intuition comes from?... Did you know your heart has more neurotransmitters than your brain? Here is how our three systems work together.

We are all familiar with the cortisol dump that happens from our brain. Our brain's job is to release hormones into our bodies to get the body to respond. Its primary function is self-preservation.

The hormones from your brain are triggered by signals sent from your heart. Your heart knows when something is going to happen before it happens! Heart Math has done a lot of research in this area, and it's phenomenal. In short, your heart will sense something ahead of time before you even know what is going to happen. Your heart sends messages to your brain to prepare for the experience, and your brain, in turn, triggers the hormones in your body to respond.

These hormones impact our physical bodies in both positive and negative ways. Often, in our noisy society, the negative is more common and what we struggle with. This is what brings on negative thoughts, feelings, and distress to our bodies. This can be from chronic illness, fatigue, lower immune systems, and other pains. Today, despite all the gyms and push towards physical health, we still continue to neglect this area.

Let's be clear about what physical health means. If you are already on your phone searching for gyms or cute workout clothes, you're doing it wrong. When I talk about physical health, we are referring to the well-being of our bodies, encompassing various elements like the food we put into it, the exercise we choose to do, and the real rest we need. It is paramount to adopt a healthy lifestyle with habits and practices; you create a harmonious environment for your body, allowing it to directly impact your spiritual growth.

I know what I'm talking about here. I was diagnosed with a variety of diseases, including fibromyalgia, rheumatoid arthritis, cancer, IBS, the list goes on. I felt like I was a walking diagnosis and trapped. Literally disabled, suicidal, isolated, and truly hopeless. Yet here I am. I came back and have a life so abundant I couldn't even have dreamt of it being possible. So, listen to me carefully when I say, I know what I'm teaching you and the process I'm taking you through. It wasn't just me I helped, I made it my mission to find hope, abundance and a life filled with purpose.

Thousands have been helped by me and my team to achieve a purposeful, blissful life. It's our mission.

When we really think about health, we think about food deprivation, skinny people, gyms, and all the things. The truth is that it comes from society. So, stop that! Stop it right now. Open your mind and continue reading to learn, think, and own this yourself.

A healthy body provides us with the necessary energy, vitality, and resilience to embark on a spiritual journey. When our physical health is robust, we are better equipped to engage in exercises, cultivating a pure mind and spirit. Meditation, awareness, and self-reflection are massive here. These activities help us develop a deeper awareness of ourselves, our emotions, and our connection to the world around us.

Let's be real here: physical health influences our mental state, which is important in nurturing spiritual growth. The mind and body are intricately connected, with each influencing the other. When our bodies are unwell, we may experience discomfort, pain, and fatigue, which can disrupt our mental and emotional well-being. Conversely, when our bodies are healthy, we are better able to tackle the challenges of spiritual growth with clarity and focus.

These physical symptoms are alarms. My teacher gave the best analogy. Our homes are where we live, create memories, and care for our needs. Many of us secure our homes with alarm systems. So, let's look at it this way. When we are having an alarm go off, we don't know where or what. We just hear the piercing noise of the alarm and must run around to figure out what caused it. Running from room to room, checking windows and doors, all the while, our brains are in hyper mode, trying to be prepared for what we find. Welp, our body's symptoms are alarms. We must track down the noise and find the cause.

Most of the time, because of pressures in life, we ignore the alarms way before we even think about solving them. We grab a quick pill for the headache, a cream for the joint, or a drink for the tension. Earplugs don't turn the alarm off, you do! All the while, more alarms are going off around us, and we later become chronically ill, diseased, or disabled and blame genetics, exposures, or some other reason instead of our own ignorance of awareness.

Having awareness and discipline is the only way to embark on a spiritual journey, along with commitment and dedication. People come to me all the time wanting spiritual growth, to be psychic, enlightened, connected. However, they aren't willing to address the fact that physical health plays a crucial role in supporting these qualities. When we prioritize our physical well-being, we cultivate discipline through regular exercise and commitment by adhering to pure, clean organic diets, and dedication by honoring our body's need for rest and rejuvenation. These qualities spill over into our spiritual endeavors as well, fostering a strong foundation for growth and development.

It is important to note that physical health is not the sole determinant of spiritual growth, but rather, it acts as an ally and support system. Our spiritual growth can be hindered if we neglect our physical health, as physical discomfort and illness have the potential to distract and derail our focus from our spiritual pursuits. This matters! Without spiritual truth, we don't find purpose. Your purpose is your true, authentic soul/spirit.

How do we do this, you ask? Even if you're not, I'm going to tell you all the things. As you can tell, this part of the journey was difficult for me. Let's rip the blindfold off, shall we…

I'm a born and natural seer (we can all do it, so don't get excited). My connection to my creator was so strong I had mad skills. I could see and hear everything, and it came in handy for the life I entered into, a life that was highly volatile; it gave me an opportunity to learn who and what not to be. As I matured, I saw something horrific I couldn't wrap my juvenile mind around. I could only think of how I never wanted to see it again. So, the very thing that was protecting me and keeping me safe, I stopped immediately.

Yes, I have healed through all this and realized what I did. But that isn't part of this story. The practices I used to heal are the practices I am teaching you in this book though.

Life moved on, and about a year later, I started getting sick. The stress mounded as I continued to be "normal". I became bulimic at first, throwing off my whole digestive system, leading to other health problems, accidents, and behaviors, partnered with addictions (I loved sweets and smoking).

Many years later, I kept pushing through life, and when my visions popped up or any sort of seeing or hearing, I pushed it away. It hurt me before, and I wasn't going to be that naive again. Well, I just kept getting sicker and having more accidents.

My wake-up call was being a single mom of two little girls with a bunch of puppies and a high-stress job. All that led to me being unconscious. No seriously, I was found unconscious and taken to the hospital.

After two years of trying all the things the doctors experimented with (while still finding new diagnoses), my rheumatologist told me I had a mind-body-spirit disconnect, and until I got that fixed, I wouldn't get better.

What the fuck! I'm a Goddamn psychic! What do you mean I have a mind-body-spirit disconnect, were my thoughts at the time. At our last appointment, she suggested I go on disability. Hearing this come out of her mouth, I was shocked and devastated. I swallowed her words and went home to melt down.

She was right though! Western medicine couldn't fix the mess I was in. I was physically dying because I chose "society", I chose to not matter, I chose to be small, disconnected…all these things!

That woman saved my life, and now we are going to make sure that this isn't your story! You are a strong, divine soul living in a human body! You are worth every raw fingertip from typing this book, every workshop, course, and speaking I do. I lose my voice, but fill your hearts and minds. The reward is high.

Okay, now that I'm crying, let's get back on track here. Where did I start? FOOD, my friend, food.

Food is energy. Not just the energy your body needs for vitality. Food absorbs energy. Our massive production of food is all a lie. First of all, we actually don't need much food for our bodies at all. The reason we eat so much is because our bodies are starving for real food!

Here is what I did. I stopped eating out. Not gonna lie, this one was hard because it's so built into our lives. You ever been asked on a date, and their intention was to take you out to dinner? Yeah, awkward stories here. Okay, I have to tell you just one really funny one real quick.

I was so excited to go on a date. It was my first one! My coworker helped me get ready, and I had the cutest dress; the weather was perfect. He took me to dinner, and now, keep in mind, I'm a vegetarian, only eat organic, and I don't drink. But what did I do... I did the "date". I ate seafood, had a few sips of wine, and pretended to be "normal". Oh my God, what a mistake! As we were leaving, I started to feel horrible. But I didn't want to ruin the night. He even asked, "Are you okay?" "Yes!" I told him, "I'm having a great time. Just a little off from dinner." The valet brought our car around and we didn't make it a mile down the road before, like a rock star, I was going to be sick. He quickly pulled over, and I vomited everywhere and passed out! This still makes me laugh so hard to this day. What was I thinking? I was thinking of all the stories and experiences I saw in shows, movies and from friends of what dates were supposed to be like. I was fitting into what the societal expectation was.

Look at what you are eating and drinking. You want to always eat organic, period. You don't want processed food in your body. Do you think your body sees a McDonald's and is like, "Hey girls, what's up. This is the most nourishing cow I can put in my mouth, and I won't need to eat again today". NO! Your body is trying to digest the "food" and pull the nutrients and energy out. What is it supposed to do with processed food? You don't want chemicals, negative energy from poor environments, or the weeks-old produce that has no nutrition left in it. Don't you deserve to have whole, nutritious, pure food? I do!

For all of you people who are like, I don't have time to cook so much, I can't find organic food, I.... whatever your excuse is. That is just an excuse. I live in the middle of nowhere. I run a company, work full time, and have a family; oh, and I'm writing this book. If it matters to you, you will do it. Just take baby steps.

I now have two grow towers in my home, and I always have fresh, beautiful, delicious foods that make my body sing. To keep it real, it took me two years to figure out a way that worked for me. Turns out the grow towers were easier than fighting the wild for my food.

Okay, we put the good food in our bodies. Our bodies are happy. What about the gym? Screw the gym, I mean really…

I had a gym membership. It was a great excuse to come home later so I didn't have to deal with the chaos eroding. Avoiding my responsibilities. Don't judge. We all have our secrets; I'm just very public about mine. Plus, it got my doctor to stop telling me to exercise. "See, I went to the gym, I have a membership."

Needless to say, the gym didn't work for what I needed. I needed a mind, body, and spirit connection.

You have two choices now. Tai Chi or Yoga... I went with yoga. Got the certifications even. Can you tell I am all in when I'm in?

Which yoga to do now? Welp, here's the deal. Just find one you like, and do it. But to help you out, here are three of my favorites and what they are roughly.

Let's start with Nidra. Nidra yoga is powerful. In our world, we could call this adult napping or guided meditations. You lay down, have guided prompts, and get up rejuvenated. Now the secret to this yoga is it's a healing yoga. Heck, even the military uses it to help the troops with PTSD. It's all about detoxifying ourselves and connecting.

Next, look at Hatha yoga. Try to stick to normal Hatha, meaning not hot yoga or something else like that. You want to move your body and connect your nervous system to yourself again. Remember those alarms you have been ignoring? Well, get ready to find the source. This was the first yoga I tried. To be honest, it was too much for my delicate system back then. I could rock this now though.

Now to my favorite yoga, Kundalini, which has become pretty popular now that people realize they need to have a spiritual connection. This yoga focuses on that. Did it fix my IBS? Yes. Did it fix my fibro? Yes. This is where I started my mind, body, and spirit connection.

I'm not saying yoga is for everyone. This is why you choose it. You can give Tai Chi a go. All I'm saying is, do something! And when I get my foot behind my head, I'll let you all know. For now, I have a new yoga practice that has given me back the mobility of my toes and fingers, and I'm loving it!

With practice, you will find you are calmer, you're connected, and your health dramatically improves.

Oh, let's not forget sleep! I mean, we do…that's the problem. We are exhausted! There are never enough hours in the day. Sleep becomes something we know we need and want. Often, it's one of the first places we sacrifice. Here is the deal: I'm going against popular recommendations of 8 hours. I'm here to say you only need about 4 to 5 hours of sleep. This only applies in one situation. You are healthy and happy, doing all the mind, body, and spirit practices I'm teaching you here. Naturally, without effort, you will simply start to need less sleep.

Settle down with the no-sleep ideas you are already conjuring up. You must earn this. Treat it like a gift. Don't abuse it. When I first started practicing yoga every morning, I was feeling better, and then, over time, for no reason, I just started sleeping less. Turns out the yogis and yoginis know this. This was so unexpected and truly a gift. After all those years of needing 10 hours or more of sleep, often only getting 2-4.

When the girls were little, I had to work a lot and sometimes would skip sleeping altogether. I'd like to say I was busy doing hot girl stuff, but I was just busy trying to keep up with the societal pressures. The girls and I went for a wellness check after my second daughter. The doctor always checked on me too, asking how much sleep I was getting. I was so exhausted; makeup couldn't even hide the evidence. When I told her I hadn't slept in a few days, she smiled and said, "Don't worry, you are fine. Just make sure you catch up." I'm sure she saw the confused and unexpected look on my face. But she assured me, "You can catch up on your sleep if you do it within three days." Well, clearly, as you saw how my life turned, I abused this information and ran myself to empty. So again, don't abuse the gift. It doesn't keep on giving unless you fill it back up.

Otherwise, yes, make sure you are getting a solid quality sleep of 8 hours a night. As you heal the whole of you, this will just naturally adjust. The first game changer to your sleep is a ritual. The ritual is important because it tells your brain to start to settle down and prepare for bed. Give yourself 20-30 minutes of a bedtime ritual. This shouldn't be difficult; some of these you might already do.

- Try drinking relaxing warm tea about 20 minutes before bed
- In the same 20 minutes, stop using blue screens (yes this is your TV, phone, tablet, etc.)

- Take a shower
- Brushing your teeth
- Set out the next day's clothes
- Water your plants
- Try reading a good ol' fashion paper book
- Meditate/Pray
- Dim the lights

I don't care what ritual you make, just make it a ritual. You will find in the same week of doing this every day that you're off to sleep much more easily.

Our connection between physical health and spiritual growth is undeniable. By being aware and taking care of our physical well-being, we create a stable and supportive environment for our spiritual endeavors. When our bodies are healthy, we have the energy, resilience, and mental clarity to embark on a journey of self-discovery and spiritual growth. It is vital to recognize the importance of maintaining physical health with our spiritual practices, as they are intrinsically intertwined in facilitating our overall well-being.

You are divine. Modern science is just now scratching the surface of understanding the beautiful complex systems we have. This is why I go back to the ancient times when people weren't following or listening based on popularity, money, or power. We visit the sages, masters, creators, our foundational wisdom we have moved so far away from.

Now that we have explored the strong correlation between physical health and spiritual growth, let's take a look at your thoughts from the list I have created to help you prioritize and nurture your physical well-being as a foundation for your spiritual journey.

Checklist:

1. **Physical Health Impact:** Reflect on the impact of your physical health on your overall well-being.
2. **Evaluate Your Physical Health:** Evaluate how nurturing your physical health can lay a solid foundation for your mental and spiritual well-being.
3. **Identify Elements:** Identify the various elements of your physical health, such as nutrition, exercise, and rest.
4. **Healthy Body Benefits:** Recognize the benefits of your healthy body, including energy, vitality, and resilience for your spiritual activities.
5. **Notice Your Discomforts:** Consider how your physical discomfort and illness(es) can disrupt your mental and emotional well-being.
6. **Reflect on Your Mental State:** Reflect on your energy, resilience, and mental clarity necessary for your self-discovery and growth.

7. **Making the Right Decisions for You:** Make decisions that prioritize and nurture your physical health alongside your spiritual practices.
8. **Always be Adjusting:** Continuously evaluate and adjust your decisions based on the connection between your physical health and spiritual growth.

I want to share a few more stories with you to help bring this home.

June practiced regular exercise and followed a nutritious diet. She experienced physical health benefits such as increased energy levels, improved sleep, and reduced stress. June was then able to dedicate more time and mental focus to her spiritual practices, such as meditation and self-reflection, leading to enhanced spiritual growth.

Jordan and Sam both engaged in spiritual practices. One of them suffered from chronic physical pain and fatigue due to poor physical health, while the other was physically fit and healthy. The person with good physical health had a clearer mind, better emotional stability, and higher levels of energy to explore and deepen her spiritual journey, bringing her more bliss in her life and the energy to be responsible for fulfilling her purpose. On the other hand, the one facing physical health issues struggled to fully engage in spiritual practices, as their focus may be divided between physical discomfort and their spiritual pursuits.

Joy neglected her physical health, indulging in an unhealthy lifestyle and lacked exercise and proper nutrition. Her physical well-being began to decline, and she constantly experienced fatigue and lethargy. As a result, she found it difficult to concentrate during meditation or engage in spiritual practices that require mental focus. Her spiritual growth was hindered because her physical health was not supporting her desired outcome.

Michelle recently started prioritizing her physical health by improving her diet and integrating regular exercise into her routine and found that her body felt lighter and more energized. This newfound physical well-being allowed her to delve deeper into her spiritual practices. Michelle could experience a sense of connection to something greater than herself and gain valuable insights during meditation and self-reflection. Not to mention the stress dissipating.

These stories highlight the relationship between physical health and spiritual growth, showing you how prioritizing physical well-being can create a conducive environment for spiritual practices, and allowing you to deepen your self-awareness and connection to the world around you.

Is that clear? There is a strong connection between physical health, mental well-being, and spiritual growth. The state of our physical well-being can greatly impact our ability to engage in and benefit from positive mental wellness and spiritual practices.

Case Study: The Impact of Physical Health on Spiritual Growth

In a small community called Harmony Valley, there was a group of individuals who were passionate about personal growth and spiritual development. They recognized the importance of physical health in supporting their spiritual journeys and decided to initiate a project to promote the mind-body-spirit connection.

The community partnered with local health professionals and opened a wellness center, offering services such as nutrition counseling, exercise classes, and holistic therapies like acupuncture and yoga. The center aimed to provide resources and support for individuals to prioritize their physical health.

They organized educational workshops on topics like the benefits of organic raw nutrition, exercise, and rest for spiritual growth. These workshops aimed to raise awareness and teach practical strategies for incorporating healthy lifestyle habits into daily routines.

To create a sense of community and accountability, they organized group activities such as group hikes, meditation sessions, and cooking classes. These activities encouraged individuals to engage in physical activities and healthy cooking, further promoting physical health and its connection to spiritual growth.

The wellness center saw a significant increase in attendance and utilization of its services. More individuals began seeking guidance and resources to improve their physical health, indicating a growing recognition of the importance of physical health in spiritual growth.

Through the workshops and group activities, participants reported making positive changes in their lifestyle habits. They started adopting healthier eating habits, engaging in regular physical exercise, and prioritizing rest and self-care. These changes were attributed to an increased understanding of the impact of physical health on their spiritual journeys.

Participants reported experiencing a deeper connection to their bodies and a greater awareness of the mind-body connection. They observed that by nurturing their physical health, they felt more grounded, centered, and present, which facilitated their spiritual growth.

It wasn't easy to start, though. Some individuals in the community initially resisted the idea of prioritizing physical health for spiritual growth, viewing it as unrelated or secondary. It required consistent education and communication efforts to overcome this resistance and shift perspectives.

The community faced challenges in securing sufficient resources to establish the wellness center and organize educational workshops. However, they overcame this limitation by leveraging local partnerships, volunteers, and grassroots fundraising efforts.

Maintaining a long-term commitment to physical health practices proved challenging for some individuals. They faced obstacles such as lack of time, motivation, or support. Regular check-ins, support groups, and personalized guidance were implemented to help individuals overcome these challenges and sustain their commitment.

Providing education and raising awareness about the mind-body-spirit connection is crucial. By providing individuals with information and practical strategies, they become more motivated to prioritize their physical health.

The sense of community and support played a vital role in encouraging people to make positive changes. Creating an environment where they could connect, share experiences, and hold each other accountable enhanced their ability to prioritize physical health.

Recognizing the interconnectedness of mind, body, and spirit is fundamental. Taking a holistic approach and integrating various practices and disciplines ensures a balanced and sustainable path towards spiritual growth.

The initiatives taken in Harmony Valley had a significant impact on the mind-body-spirit connection. By prioritizing physical health, individuals in the community experienced tangible benefits in their spiritual growth and becoming their authentic selves. They developed a deeper awareness of themselves and enhanced their discipline and commitment, cultivating a stronger foundation for personal growth. The initiatives served as a catalyst, elevating the understanding and recognition of the mind-body-spirit connection in the community, and paving the way for continued growth and development.

Now that you have processed all these examples and their impact on the mind-body-spirit connection in Harmony Valley, let's look at the common mistakes to avoid when implementing similar initiatives. These mistakes can hinder your effectiveness and progress in promoting physical health for spiritual growth.

Based on my experience, one mistake that most people make is neglecting their physical health while focusing solely on their spiritual growth. This is just silly. Yet, I see it all the time. I know a lot of readers and spiritual people; trust me when I say this again; I see it all the time. Your soul/spirit lives in your body. If you don't care for your body, and its energy isn't functioning properly, how do you expect to have a good connection?

Look at it through the Chakras. We have 7 main ones that most of us are familiar with. Chakras are literally an energy source that travels through our bodies, just like our blood, oxygen, and nervous system. These energy fields need to flow and be able to connect. If you are all buggered up, how do you expect them to be connecting when the channels are blocked? Imagine what happens to your spiritual journey when they are open and flowing beautifully like they were intended.

This can be avoided by recognizing the importance of maintaining physical health alongside spiritual practices. Prioritizing your health, creating a stable foundation for spiritual growth. Acknowledge the connection between your physical health and mental state. This can help you avoid the mistake you have read about here. Say no to illness, disease, and chronic problems stopping you from reaching your full potential.

Focus on self-care and prioritize activities that nourish your mind, body, and spirit daily.

Here is what I shared:

- Nurturing your physical health gives you a solid foundation for your spiritual growth.

- A healthy body provides the energy and resilience needed for a meaningful spiritual journey.
- Prioritizing your physical health cultivates discipline, commitment, and dedication, essential qualities for spiritual growth.
- Your physical well-being supports mental and emotional well-being, needed aspects of nurturing your spiritual growth.
- Recognize the undeniable connection between physical health and spiritual growth to create overall well-being.

Let's dig in!

Find your pen or pencil. It's time for you to do some work now.

1. How is your connection between your physical health and spiritual growth?

_____
_____
_____
_____

2. What does your physical health look like now?

_____
_____
_____
_____

3. How does your physical health support your spiritual growth?

_____
_____
_____
_____

4. What are you going to start doing this week?

_____
_____
_____
_____

5. How does your physical health influence your mental state?

_____
_____
_____
_____

6. What do you need to change to embark on a spiritual journey?

_____
_____
_____
_____

7. How does physical health assist with these changes?

_____
_____
_____
_____

8. What is the potential impact of neglecting your physical health?

_____
_____
_____
_____

9. How are physical health and spiritual growth intrinsically intertwined?

_____
_____
_____
_____

See, it's getting better. You are connecting the pieces. Now, let's venture into the next chapter, where we will delve into the realm of simple yet transformative practices to further enhance our spiritual growth – practices that will truly ignite your inner light.

Chapter 3

The Transformation Begins: Simple Yet Powerful Practices for Spiritual Growth

"Enlightenment is an ordinary life lived in an extraordinary way!"

– Swami Nithyananda

- Discover the power of mindful breathing to find calm and presence amid chaos.
- Unleash your inner thoughts and emotions through the transformative practice of journaling.
- Embrace gratitude to shift your perspective and cultivate a deep sense of appreciation and abundance.
- Find balance and inner peace through mindful movement practices like yoga, Tai Chi, and Qi Gong.
- Tap into the healing power of nature to nurture your spirit, find solace, and be inspired by the beauty that surrounds you.

I understand that many individuals seeking spiritual growth are in a place of unhappiness and hopelessness. Feeling empty and alone. Spiritual practices are being craved now by many because of the realization of the fulfillment it brings, leading to our authentic selves.

It is important to remember that realizing you are not alone and recognizing your personal power is a crucial step in your journey. To transform your spiritual well-being, I would like to introduce you to some simple yet impactful practices that can lead you towards a path of growth and self-discovery. Getting you on a path in general to spiritual growth and the ability to continue this beautiful lifelong journey.

Oh, and hold for a hot second. Before I start diving in with my opinions and teachings. Let me start by saying this is not about "converting" you or any particular spiritual belief. I leave these choices to you. I'm sharing what has worked. At least the start of you finding connection.

Can I just start by saying the word "mindfulness" drives me up the wall. Mind-Fulness. I process this with the mind is full and lacking focus. That is a piece of our complexity. Not the whole…We have thousands and thousands of people running around teaching meditation and other ancient practices (like yoga) without a guru or the knowings of the full experience. The intentions and spiritual teachings have been drawn out of them, lowering their powerful manifestation that happens within. But don't worry. I got you. And if you are looking for a guru, let me know. I'm happy to point you to where you need to go.

Let's call it as it is. Meditation. I think this changed because so many people said, "I can't meditate". So, to get around it they made a bunch of stuff up.

The reality is I was that person! There was no way I was giving up the noise in my head. I had too much going on and had to keep up. What I didn't know was the damage being done and how much I truly needed this peace. I found the "mindfulness" wasn't what I was "seeking". I was seeking a spiritual connection, to fill my loneliness and having something higher than myself to believe in. No one told me this mindfulness stuff was the gateway. But it got me to stop and finally try it for 5 minutes.

Breathing is clearly part of the whole thing. On a scientific level, breathing is what controls our brain's ability to realize. For example, when you increase your breath, your body responds by increasing activity and releasing hormones for the situation. We have breathing for all the things! I'm going to give you a few practices to try on your own in our daily situations that can occur.

Here is what I use whenever anyone is new and texts in a panic. Box breathing. It's simple and it works. If you can count to 4 you got this. Close your eyes. Take a deep breath in for 4 seconds, hold for 4 seconds, release for 4 seconds, and hold again for 4 seconds. Do these steps three to five times and you will quickly find your brain calms down and you can process much better. See that one wasn't so hard now was it.

One of the simplest and most accessible practices is breath awareness. Take a few moments each day to focus your attention on your breath. Close your eyes, inhale deeply through your nose, feel your breath through your throat, chest and abdomen, and exhale slowly through your mouth, feeling your body relax. Shoulders dropping, hips releasing, feet and hands becoming heavy and limp. This practice helps to center your mind, calm your nervous system, and bring you into the present moment. Over time, it allows you to develop a deeper connection with yourself and the world around you.

This one is my favorite "gateway" if you will, and what I teach for anyone beginning. A 20-minute morning and evening meditation. Start by settling down by using the technique above. As thoughts pop into your mind, let them slowly disappear and fade away.

Focus on one thing. A prayer, chant, mantra, whichever you pick for this session, stick to it. An easy one is to say to yourself in your head, "I am aware of my body; I smile at my body" for 10 minutes. On the second half, you can say to yourself something like, "I am aware of my heart; I smile at my heart". As you become more practiced you can hold one thought for 20 minutes.

To go deeper, you do need a teacher. Because in the spiritual world, you get initiated into practice. Meaning the divine delivers you a unique and specific practice. These initiations are often private, and you are encouraged to not share your sacred practice. This is why we only go this deep in publications because you must start your own journey into spirituality and your connection to know. Of course, this is the path I took and continue to grow along.

Meditation is proven to build our connection. Calming our bodies, quieting our minds, and filling our spirit. It increases our awareness and opens our 3rd eye as well. I do this twice a day and love it!

If you want to be guided through this journey, download our app, Journeying with Jessica. I have meditations recorded for free there. When you are ready, I strongly recommend TM.org for a deeper meditation practice that will change your world.

Finding your own path can be a challenge. Regardless of your beliefs, you must find someone who is authentic, lives this life and can truly guide you where you need to go.

I have practiced a variety of Christianity, Paganism, Hinduism, and even Buddhism. All in search of finding what aligned with me. I have some students who mix it all up and practice many of these beliefs to continue their spiritual growth, while others focus on one. This is your journey, own it.

Another powerful practice is regular journaling. Something I also used to despise. If someone told me to journal, I would pretty much vent into my phone and consider it done. Here's the deal. You actually have to write. Pen to paper. It's about using your hand to write. It's opening that other part of our brain. That is why you see at the end of every chapter, I ask you thought-provoking questions.

What to write is the question. You can google journal writing prompts and knock yourself out. Or you can use what I do. In the morning, I write about my night, and in the evening, welp, I write about my day. Now I'm not writing about what I ate, drank, or who I saw. No, I'm writing specifically about points that stood out in the day. What made me happy, what bothered me. That's it. Then I take that information and use it for my meditation.

See how I just did that. Merge the practices together. That is how they were originally designed, for a reason. Now you will want to know about the meditation part. I'll give you a high-level overview because you are going to learn this practice in another chapter. I call it pattern digging.

The positive points I store and smile over. Sending my energy of gratitude where it needs to go for that experience. The lower points or spots where I thought, "That's not right". I revisit the experience as many times as I need to allow myself to release it.

Keep in mind this whole thing is just a few minutes. Maybe give 5 minutes to write and 5-10 to process/meditate. You can adjust the time as you need. Often, people start with 30 minutes until you get the hang of it.

Commit to setting aside a dedicated time each day to reflect on your thoughts, emotions, and experiences. Write freely without judgment or expectation, allowing your innermost thoughts and feelings to flow onto the paper. This process helps you gain insight, release pent-up emotions, and develop self-awareness. By exploring your thoughts and experiences through journaling, you can uncover patterns, identify areas for growth, and cultivate a sense of clarity and purpose.

Growing a regular gratitude practice is a transformative way to shift your perspective and promote spiritual growth. This is why when journaling, I also write gratitude. Begin or end each day by writing down three things you are grateful for. These can be simple pleasures or significant events.

Recently, at a weeklong conference, there was no food I could eat. Even the salads they served had foods outside my diet or I was allergic to ingredients. On day two of not eating, I finally found something. I was so grateful. My gratitude practice each day was dedicated to how grateful I was to them.

By focusing on what you are thankful for, you shift your attention away from negativity and scarcity and, instead, embrace an attitude of abundance and appreciation. Regularly acknowledging the blessings in your life helps to increase your overall sense of well-being and fosters a deeper connection to the world around you.

Bonus here: your thoughts, feelings and actions are energy. Every moment, engagement, and experience is messaging. Thinking about these moments, penning them down, and spending time on them puts that positive energy back out in the world. Manifesting more greatness, love, and connection. Spread the love.

Look at you, you beautiful soul, sending so much happiness out in the world!

Let's look at the partnership with your daily yoga, Tai Chi, or Qi Gong, which can also greatly contribute to spiritual growth. These practices promote physical health and flexibility and encourage mental and emotional balance. Through intentional and focused movement, you cultivate awareness of your body, breath, and sensations. This deepens your connection to your physical self and helps you become more present in the moment.

The impact of physical fitness on mental and emotional health cannot be overstated. Engaging in regular exercise benefits our physical well-being and has profound effects on our mental and emotional states. The mind-body connection is a powerful tool, and yoga, in particular, can be a transformative practice for those seeking to improve their mental and emotional well-being.

There are so many benefits of physical fitness on mental and emotional health. Firstly, exercise releases endorphins, which are neurotransmitters that promote feelings of happiness and well-being. These endorphins act as natural painkillers and mood stimulants, effectively countering stress, anxiety, and even symptoms of depression.

Physical fitness has been shown to reduce levels of cortisol, also known as the stress hormone. High levels of cortisol can contribute to feelings of anxiety and tension, negatively impacting mental and emotional health. By engaging in regular exercise, we can effectively lower cortisol levels, promoting a sense of calm and stability.

In terms of incorporating exercise into daily routines, it is crucial to find activities that resonate with you and fit your lifestyle. Clearly, I promote yoga. If you want to experience the mental and emotional benefits of exercise, yoga is for you. Yoga not only enhances physical strength, flexibility, and balance but also fosters a deep mind-body-spirit connection.

Tips for starting:

Work your way into it by starting with a 30-minute practice and increasing from there. My morning yoga is now 90 minutes long and at a fast pace. This is not where I started! I started with 30 minutes and a slow pace. This allowed me to gently improve my connection and process.

Pick a time to do this every morning. I start mine at 5 am. It is best to start your day with your practice. The first week, you will have to force yourself to do it. But then it becomes something you crave and need to have a peaceful day without pains, lack of focus, and calmness of balanced emotions.

Set aside a quiet, clutter-free area in your home where you can practice. Having a designated space creates a sense of stability and allows you to fully immerse yourself in your practice.

Beginning in the present moment is critical for spiritual growth. The Universe (I'm going to use that word instead of listing off all the possible beliefs and practices; you're welcome) speaks softly and gently. We might not be gentle with ourselves, but the universe is because it knows just how delicate we are.

Living in the past keeps us stuck from moving forward. Being human, we often focus on the negative. So, looking back isn't helping you any, that time has already passed. Looking forward typically brings anxiety and missing out on the present moment. The present moment is where the magic is. Slow down, be present, be aware. If you only knew how many signs were being communicated to you each day. It's pure bliss when you are in the present moment and open to receiving.

With daily practice, you will experience increased vitality, a sense of inner peace, and a greater understanding of your body-mind connection. And the calmness, oh the calmness of integrating all of this is magical.

The connections are all around us. We just need to slow down and absorb them. Being outside is a part of this. Do you go outside? This is a legit question. Lots of people don't go outside, or if they do it's while they are running to the car, to the market, to work, or well, running somewhere. But do you ever go outside and just be there?

The most glorious creations are right here in front of our own eyes every day. We hear the birds, feel the air, smell the water, and indulge in a massive array of colors. It's magnificent.

Spending time in nature is an essential practice for promoting spiritual growth. It literally rejuvenates your soul, grounds you to earth, and feeds your beings.

Take regular walks in a park, sit by a lake, or hike in the mountains. Allow yourself to be fully present in the natural environment, noticing the sights, sounds, and sensations around you. Connecting with nature helps you tap into a deeper sense of interconnectedness and reminds you of the beauty and vastness of the world. It can offer moments of solace, awe, and inspiration, nurturing your spirit and providing a grounding foundation for growth. A few times a day, I step outside and just bask in its glory. Taking it all in. In the morning, I find myself smiling while watching the world wake up.

Remember, these practices are simple, yet their effects can be transformative when embraced with consistency and dedication. Incorporate them into your daily routine, even if only for a few minutes at a time. And for the love of all creation, don't try to do these all at once! Take it in little steps, feel it out, and enjoy. As you embark on this spiritual journey, believe in your own power, have faith in the process, and trust that the smallest of steps will lead you towards significant growth.

I want you to enjoy this journey. Take your time to meet the authentic you, and connect with the whole you. This leads you to your purpose and fulfillment in life. If you get stuck or find that you need support, we are here. For years, I have been teaching everything in this book. We have communities for you, practices, and ongoing teachings to help you on the journey to your full potential.

Now that you have read about these impactful practices for spiritual growth, I invite you to start thinking. This checklist will serve as a helpful guide for incorporating these practices into your daily routine and embracing your own spiritual journey.

Checklist:

1. Meditation:

- Find a quiet and comfortable space.
- Sit in a relaxed posture; keep your back straight but comfortable and close your eyes.
- Focus on your breath, observing each inhalation and exhalation.
- Let go of thoughts as they arise and bring your attention back to your breath.
- Practice 1-2 times a day to increase self-awareness, calmness, and a deeper connection with your inner self.

2. Gratitude Practice:

- Reflect on things you are grateful for each day.

- Appreciate simple things like a beautiful sunrise or a helpful gesture from someone.
- Consider writing down your gratitude in a journal to amplify the practice and maintain focus on the positive aspects of your life.

3. Daily Affirmations:

- Choose empowering affirmations that resonate with you. These are your mantras you create.
- Repeat these affirmations daily to shift your mindset and reinforce positive beliefs.
- Consistent practice can lead to a rewiring of your patterns, resulting in a shift in thoughts, emotions, and actions.

4. Journaling:

- Dedicate a few minutes each day to writing your experiences in a journal.
- Gain clarity about what is truly important to you.
- Uncover inner wisdom and identify patterns that may be holding you back, fostering personal growth and spiritual development.

5. Nature Connection:

- Spend time in nature regularly.
- Take walks in the park, spend time near a body of water, or sit under a tree.

- Engage all your senses and appreciate the beauty and harmony of the natural world.
- Ground yourself and cultivate a sense of awe and wonder, facilitating spiritual growth.

6. Remember:

- Consistency and commitment are key to the transformative power of these practices.
- Incorporate them into your daily routine.
- Approach them with patience and an open mind.
- Trust in the process and take small steps every day.

These guidelines provide a starting point for your spiritual journey. If you have further questions or need additional guidance, feel free to ask.

Case Study: Transforming Spiritual Well-being through Mindfulness and Practices

Jane is a great example to share around this. A 35-year-old woman who was feeling lost and disconnected in her life. She was unhappy with her job, had recently ended a long-term relationship, and was struggling to find meaning and purpose. She sought guidance and support to cultivate her spiritual well-being and embark on a journey of self-discovery.

Jane incorporated mindful breathing into her daily routine. Every morning and evening, she set aside five minutes to focus on her breath, allowing herself to center her mind and be present in the moment.

She also committed to journaling for 15 minutes each night. She wrote freely about her thoughts, emotions, and experiences, being sure to note her gratitude for her experience each day. This helped to shift her perspective and cultivate an attitude of abundance and appreciation. Creating an opportunity for self-reflection and gaining insights into her life.

Attending weekly yoga classes and incorporating short exercises into her daily routine, she focused on her body, breath, and sensations during these practices, allowing herself to develop a deeper connection with her physical self and improve her mobility.

Often not making time to be outside, Jane made it a priority to spend time in nature regularly. She took long walks in the park, sat by the beach, and went hiking on weekends. During these moments, she immersed herself in the beauty and tranquility of the natural environment, fostering a sense of connection and awe.

Adapting these changes over the weeks, Jane experienced a massive transformation. Gaining a deeper understanding of herself, her desires, and her experiences. She became more aware of her patterns, triggers, and areas for growth.

She noticed a significant shift in her overall sense of well-being. She felt calmer, more grounded, and experienced a greater sense of peace and contentment in her daily life.

By embracing gratitude and connecting with nature, Jane developed a more positive outlook on life. She found joy and appreciation in the simple pleasures and felt a greater sense of interconnectedness with the world around her.

Some areas Jane struggled with along the way included maintaining consistency in her daily practices. At times, she found it challenging to prioritize her spiritual growth amidst her busy schedule. She faced occasional setbacks but remained committed to her journey.

For many of us, change is difficult. Initially, Jane faced resistance and skepticism towards these practices. It took time for her to integrate and embrace them fully to overcome her skepticism.

As she continued to grow one little step at a time, Jane realized that consistent small actions had a powerful impact on her spiritual well-being. She learned to appreciate the importance of patience and persistence in her journey.

Jane discovered the importance of adapting practices to her preferences and needs. She experimented with different techniques and found what resonated with her the most.

Jane's spiritual practices and growth initiatives had a profound impact on her life. She experienced a deeper connection with herself, a greater sense of well-being, and a more positive perspective. These practices allowed her to navigate life's challenges with more grace and resilience and empowered her to embrace her personal power and find meaning and purpose. Jane continues on her spiritual journey, engaging in these practices consistently, and looks forward to further growth and self-discovery.

I love these stories because we have all been there. The stuff you are made of comes through when changing your lifestyle against societal pressures. It's easy to fall back, quit, or cheat. And by cheating, I don't mean sick. If you are sick, you need rest. That's real. To elaborate on this more, here are some examples of common challenges.

- Believing you are alone on your journey towards spiritual growth.
- Not recognizing your personal power.
- Neglecting to practice meditation as a way to center their mind and bring them into the present moment.
- Not incorporating regular journaling to gain insight, release emotions, and develop self-awareness.
- Forgetting to cultivate a regular gratitude practice to shift perspective and promote spiritual growth.

- Ignoring the benefits of mindful movement practices such as yoga, Tai Chi, or Qi Gong, for physical, mental, and emotional balance.
- Not spending time in nature to tap into a deeper sense of interconnectedness and find solace, awe, and inspiration.

Wanna know how to avoid these mistakes?

- Recognize that you are not alone and seek support and connection with others on your spiritual journey. There are hundreds of thousands of people taking this journey now.
- Embrace and believe in your personal power to create positive change.
- Set aside time each day for meditation exercises to center your mind and stay present.
- Establish a regular journaling practice to gain insight and develop self-awareness.
- Incorporate a daily gratitude practice to shift your perspective and cultivate appreciation.
- Engage in mindful movement practices to promote your mind-body-spirit connection.
- Make a conscious effort to spend time in nature often to nurture your spirit and find inspiration.

It's imperative to NOT compare your spiritual journey with others - focus on your own progress, embrace self-compassion, and trust that growth unfolds uniquely for everyone.

Now you're going to realize that you are not alone and that you possess the power to transform your spiritual well-being and world. Take a few moments each day to focus on your breath, center your mind, and bring yourself into the present moment. Reflect on your thoughts, emotions, and experiences through writing to gain insight, release pent-up emotions, and develop self-awareness. Write down three things you are grateful for each day to shift your perspective, embrace abundance, and increase your overall well-being. Spend time in nature to tap into a sense of interconnectedness, find solace and inspiration, and nurture your spirit.

Remember, even the smallest steps can lead to significant growth.

Ready to dig?

1. Are you doing any of these practices now and maybe not realizing it or doing it with intention?

_____
_____
_____
_____

2. What is your plan to implement these changes into your daily life?

_____
_____
_____
_____

3. How will this plan support your goal to live a more blissful abundant life filled will purpose?

_____
_____
_____
_____

4. Which of these are you most interested in trying? Yoga, Tai Chi, or Qi Gong.

___

5. What does your life look like once you have these implemented? Think of how you will feel physically and mentally, about your relationship changes, and the way you see the day.

___

As we explore various practices that foster spiritual growth, we soon realize the significance of maintaining inner motivation and staying committed to our personal development. In the next chapter, we delve into guiding principles and valuable insights that will inspire and encourage you to continue on this transformative journey towards self-improvement to your true potential. Keep reading to discover the keys to unlocking your own potential and nurturing lasting growth within.

Chapter 4

Finding Your Inner Drive: Uncovering Motivation for Personal Growth

"Success is not the key to happiness. Happiness is the key to success. If you love what you are doing, you will be successful."

- Albert Schweitzer

- Embark on a transformative journey of personal growth and discover the power of finding inner motivation.
- Learn practical steps to stay committed to personal growth and achieve your long-term desires.
- Create a vision board or journal to visually represent your aspirations and enhance your commitment to personal growth.
- Develop a routine and cultivate a supportive environment to fuel your motivation and maintain your dedication.

- Celebrate your milestones and progress along the way to stay committed and motivated on your personal growth journey.

I'm here for it! Say it with me: "I'm Here For It!" Let's talk about what is already popping up in your head. How to stay motivated. You are going to need to find your inner motivation and stay committed to your personal growth. Taking action is not negotiable when it comes to you living your true potential; it's necessary and a transformative journey. It requires self-reflection, dedication, and perseverance, but with the right approach, you can release yourself from your programming and take control of designing a new, blissful future. Allow me to step up on this soap box again. My polite way of saying, let me tell you my opinion...

First and foremost, let's address the importance of finding inner motivation. See, I find that people often think they are motivated. And you are, but where is the intention and focus? Let's study this for a hot minute. Motivation, at its core, stems from a deep understanding of our desires and aspirations. Do you desire a million dollars? Cool, the lottery is in business because you aren't the only one. But dig deeper. Where is your why in this bundle of cash?

You can have a money goal because, in our society, we need money to achieve success. You need to hear that again. In our society, we need money to achieve success. Can I just say this is false. What you need is a desire so powerful and so strong that it motivates you to get up at 4 in the morning to start your day. If your desires, goals, ambitions aren't doing this for you. You are focused on the wrong thing.

Take some time to reflect upon your values, passions, and long-term desires. What truly drives you? What brings you joy and contentment? What is the fire inside you burning for? When you have a clear sense of purpose, it becomes easier to stay motivated even when faced with obstacles. Now, put that nugget in the back of your head while we discuss some options.

One effective way to find inner motivation is to create a vision board or journal. These are so popular. Turns out when you make one, your success rate is like 90%! You must look at it every day. Own it! This allows you to visually represent your desires and dreams, making them more tangible. Add pictures, quotes, or anything that resonates with you. Place this vision board where it's in your face every day, such as in your bedroom or workspace, to provide a constant reminder of your aspirations. It doesn't need to be fancy if you don't want. I have a doodle. By regularly engaging with your vision board or journal, you reinforce your commitment to personal growth. It's subtle programming.

Start with a small desire or focus. For instance, instead of changing your whole diet, just try eating one thing a day that you would like to start eating. I seriously wanted to eat celery. I can't stand celery, just so we are clear. But I knew the health benefits of it and really wanted to make sure I was doing all the things. So now every day, I make a smoothie. Yep, I cover that celery in blueberries, strawberries, and bananas. It's amazing, probably because my smoothies taste like a milkshake. But hey, a girls gotta do what a girls gotta do. I eat one stick of raw organic celery every day now! You do you!

But motivation alone is not enough; you must know why you are doing it. Staying committed to personal growth requires consistent effort and dedication. Remember the last chapter: integrate slowly, no firehoses here. If you want change to take place and stick, you can't just do it all today. You take your "big" goal and break it down into smaller pieces so you can achieve it easily, and it's not overwhelming.

Here are some practical steps to help you maintain your commitment.

Establishing clear and specific desires is essential for your personal growth. Break down your long-term visions into smaller, manageable milestones. By achieving these smaller desires, you'll gain a sense of accomplishment, which will fuel your motivation and reinforce your commitment.

For example, if your long-term vision is to start your own business, set smaller desires such as researching your target market, developing a business plan, taking more courses, meeting business owners in similar markets, or taking business courses. Each completed desire brings you closer to your ultimate dream.

Consistency is key to personal growth. Create a daily or weekly routine that incorporates activities and habits aligned with your desires. This could include dedicated time for learning, physical exercise, meditation, or any other practice that contributes to your personal growth. When these activities become an integral part of your routine, they become a natural extension of who you are, helping you maintain your commitment. Something I found that worked for me was utilizing my Outlook calendar. I scheduled everything. I made notes, links and reminders for all the things so then I don't have to waste my time looking for something or deciding what to do next. The time is already set aside. Just follow the plan. You need 21 days for the memory to stick and become you. So whatever your routine is, know you have to keep it up for 21 days straight. Then it becomes you.

Yes, here we are again. Seeing patterns. Just in case you didn't hear me before…Surround yourself with like-minded individuals who support your personal growth journey. Seek out mentors, coaches, or communities that align with your interests and aspirations. Engaging with others who share similar desires can provide valuable insights, encouragement, and accountability. Additionally, consider minimizing exposure to negative influences or individuals who drain your energy. Creating a stable and supportive environment will significantly enhance your commitment to personal growth.

Let's visit this last bit. In the beginning, you are going to find that you might have a lot of negative people around you. Now how to break up? That's often the hard part. Hell, sometimes they aren't even negative, they just aren't vibing with you anymore as your vibration increases. It's cool. One of two things will happen.

Some of these people will make the choice on their own. Maybe it's because they need negativity to keep going; we know these drama mamas. When you aren't feeding them anymore, they just go find someone else to fill their need. They also might realize you aren't feeding them anymore and that you are positive and improving yourself. This relationship often evolves on its own this way, and they start to mirror your behavior. And in this case, girl, You Are Out Here Changing Lives!!

In many cases, you must break up. This doesn't have to be a "it's not you, it's me". Oddly enough, that might be the case, but you get my point. Now you have some choices to make. You can either tell them you are renovating your life and just don't have time now; you all can catch up later. Or you can simply share your feelings with them about how you need positive, supportive people around you because your vibe is going high, and you need someone who is going to encourage you to keep going.

I think it's a good time to point out that we don't turn our backs on people just because their vibe is low. We listen, support, and don't get sucked in it with them. When someone is emotionally distorted, needs to vent, or experiencing some other emotion, I listen. But then I'm putting my coaching hat on and am not attached to the situation or emotions being projected. I ask for divine support to guide my words to help them move forward.

Regularly take time to reflect on your progress, challenges, and areas for improvement. Self-reflection helps you understand your strengths and weaknesses, enabling you to adapt your strategies and make necessary adjustments. It also fosters self-awareness, which is crucial for staying committed to personal growth. Journaling, meditation, or seeking feedback from trusted individuals can facilitate this important practice. See how easy this is! I already told you to do this! I love how the blocks build and support the process.

Acknowledge and celebrate your achievements, no matter how small or big they may be. Recognizing your growth and progress reinforces your commitment and motivates you to continue pushing forward. Reward yourself with something meaningful to mark your milestones, such as treating yourself to a small indulgence or taking time for self-care. Celebrating milestones is a powerful way to stay committed to personal growth.

Remember, finding inner motivation and staying committed to personal growth is a unique and personal journey. It requires patience, resilience, and dedication. It's important to recognize that setbacks and challenges are normal parts of the process. However, by following these guidelines, cultivating a stable and supportive environment, and incorporating them into your daily life, you will pave the way for a blissful future of personal growth and achievement. Trust the process, believe in yourself, and the results will follow.

Now that you've read about finding inner motivation and staying committed to personal growth, it's time to put these strategies into action. I have created a checklist that will guide you through the steps mentioned, helping you stay on track and achieve your personal growth desires. Using this checklist, you can take control of designing a new, blissful future.

Checklist

1. **Don't cheat yourself:** you MUST Identify your values, passions, and long-term desires to gain a clear sense of purpose and inner motivation.

2. **Create the visual:** Create a vision board or journal to visually represent your desires and dreams, keeping them tangible and constantly reminding yourself of your aspirations.

3. **Breaking it down:** Break down your long-term visions into smaller, manageable desires to stay committed and motivated.

4. **Routine matters:** Develop a daily or weekly routine that incorporates activities and habits aligned with your desires to maintain consistency and progress.

5. **Like-Minded people:** Surround yourself with like-minded individuals who support your personal growth journey for valuable insights, encouragement, and accountability.

6. **Manage your energy:** Minimize exposure to negative influences or individuals who drain your energy to cultivate a supportive environment.

7. **Reflect:** Regularly practice self-reflection to understand your progress, challenges, and areas for improvement.

8. **Don't forget to celebrate:** Celebrate your achievements, no matter how small, to reinforce your commitment and motivation to continue pushing forward.
9. **Setbacks happen:** Embrace setbacks and challenges as normal parts of the process and use them as opportunities for growth and learning.
10. **Trust and believe:** Trust the process, believe in yourself, and stay dedicated to your personal growth journey for a blissful future of achievement and fulfillment.

Here are several examples to further bring this home:

Let's say your long-term desire is to run a marathon. Reflecting on your deep desire to challenge yourself physically, improve your health, and accomplish something significant can serve as your inner motivation. Visualize crossing the finish line, feeling a sense of pride and accomplishment. This inner drive will push you to stick to your training regimen, even on days when you feel tired or unmotivated.

To stay committed to personal growth, you set a clear and specific desire to read one personal development book each month. Breaking it down into smaller milestones, you commit to reading 30 minutes every day. By consistently dedicating time to reading, you become more knowledgeable, gain valuable insights, and reinforce your commitment to personal growth.

Imagine you want to enhance your creativity and artistic skills. You establish a routine of spending 30 minutes every morning engaging in a creative activity such as painting, writing, or playing a musical instrument. By incorporating this practice into your daily routine, you develop a habit of nurturing your creativity, which leads to personal growth in this area.

Suppose you aspire to become a successful entrepreneur. You actively seek out networking events, join entrepreneurship groups, and connect with mentors who have achieved the same desire. By surrounding yourself with individuals who share similar aspirations and experiences, you create an environment that supports your personal growth and provides valuable guidance and accountability.

As you embark on your personal growth journey, you regularly reflect on your progress and challenges. For example, you may journal about your daily experiences, recognize areas where you have grown, identify obstacles you've overcome, and note any patterns or behaviors that may hinder your progress. This self-reflection helps you continuously adapt your strategies and stay committed to personal growth.

Let's say your desire is to improve your public speaking skills. Each week, you challenge yourself to speak in front of a small group, gradually increasing the size and complexity of your presentations. When you accomplish a significant milestone, such as delivering a successful presentation to a large audience, you treat yourself to a special dinner or a weekend getaway. Celebrating these milestones reinforces your commitment and motivates you to continue pushing yourself.

These examples demonstrate the practical application of the concepts discussed and show how they can be tailored to various personal growth desires.

Most people make the mistake of not finding inner motivation and not staying committed to personal growth. They can avoid these mistakes by taking the following steps:

1. Reflect on your desires, values, and long-term desires to understand what truly drives you and brings you joy.
2. Create a vision board or journal to visually represent your desires and dreams, and place it in a prominent place as a constant reminder.
3. Set clear and specific desires, breaking down long-term visions into smaller, manageable milestones.
4. Develop a routine that incorporates activities and habits aligned with your desires to maintain consistency.

5. Surround yourself with like-minded individuals who support your personal growth journey.
6. Practice self-reflection regularly to understand your progress, challenges, and areas for improvement.
7. Celebrate your achievements, no matter how small, to reinforce your commitment and motivation.

By following these guidelines, cultivating a supportive environment, and incorporating them into your daily life, individuals can stay committed to personal growth and achieve a blissful future.

With these common mistakes to avoid in mind, it is important to note that individuals can greatly benefit from a core piece of advice: finding inner motivation and staying committed to personal growth.

Learn to reframe negative situations and thoughts into more positive and empowering perspectives, ultimately shifting your mindset towards hope and motivation.

Here is what we covered:

- **Take time to reflect**: Reflect on your values, passions, and long-term desires to find inner motivation and purpose.
- **Create a vision board or journal:** Visually represent your desires and dreams, making them more tangible and reminding yourself of your aspirations.

- **Set clear and specific desires:** Break your desires down into smaller milestones, and celebrate your achievements along the way.
- **Develop a routine:** Incorporating activities and habits aligned with your desires to maintain consistency and commitment to personal growth.
- **Surround yourself with like-minded individuals who support your journey:** practice self-reflection, and adapt your strategies to stay committed and motivated. Remember to celebrate your progress and trust the process.

Your turn:

1. What are your values?

_____
_____
_____
_____

2. What is your burning desire motivating you?

_____
_____
_____
_____

3. What are some practical steps for you to help keep you motivated and committed to your growth?

_____
_____
_____
_____

4. What is one way to make your desires more tangible?

_____
_____
_____
_____

5. What is important for you to trust and believe in when finding inner motivation and staying committed to personal growth?

_____
_____
_____
_____

6. Who in your life can you share your insights, encouragement, and accountability with?

_____
_____

7. What should be minimized when seeking to stay committed to personal growth?

_____

_____

_____

8. What is essential for your personal growth?

_____

_____

_____

As you reflect on the strategies for finding inner motivation and staying committed to personal growth, it becomes evident that self-care and self-love are vital components in this pursuit. In the next chapter, we will delve into the significance of prioritizing your well-being and nurturing a positive relationship with yourself to achieve a healthier and more fulfilling lifestyle, so keep reading to uncover invaluable insights for your journey.

Chapter 5

Embrace Your Beautiful Self: Cultivating Self-Love and Compassion towards Oneself

"In a society that profits from your self-doubt, liking yourself is a rebellious act."

- Caroline Caldwell

- Discover the power of self-care: Learn how prioritizing your needs can lead to a healthier lifestyle and overall well-being.
- Unleash your mental and emotional potential: Explore techniques to manage stress, anxiety, and depression and develop resilience for a positive mindset.
- Build stronger relationships: Learn how self-care and self-love can help set boundaries and attract healthier connections with others.
- Empower yourself for personal growth: Gain self-awareness, live authentically, and embark on a fulfilling journey of personal growth and self-actualization.

Self-care and self-love sounds so "squishy". This is honestly a massive part of what we have wrong with society. It's crucial to practice, achieve and maintain a healthier lifestyle. In today's fast-paced and demanding world, it is easy to neglect ourselves amidst the noise of daily life. It's essential to recognize that taking care of ourselves mentally, spiritually, and physically is the foundation for overall well-being.

Self-care involves intentionally prioritizing our own needs and engaging in activities that promote our spiritual, physical, and mental health. It is not selfish! It's a necessary practice that allows you to recharge and replenish your energy. When you neglect self-care, you run the risk of burning out, experiencing chronic stress or illness, and being disconnected from your loved ones and alone. I see this too often; I know what I'm talking about.

Embracing self-love is an integral part of your self-care. It involves cultivating a deep sense of love, acceptance, and compassion towards yourself. By practicing self-love, we develop a strong sense of self-worth and establish healthy boundaries. How many of you can use some of that? Be honest.

When you truly love yourself, you are less likely to seek validation and approval from others, becoming less disturbed by their thoughts and actions. You become free to be your authentic self and empowered by your own truth.

Prioritize you! Create a stable and supportive environment for personal growth and fulfillment. I'm not talking about indulgence; what we are told is self-care. Society would like you to believe that self-care and self-love are purchased. Meaning through spas, material purchases, and eating all the things. No. You must properly understand what self-care and self-love are for you and practice that! Let's dive in:

Taking time for self-care activities such as practicing meditation and journaling, engaging in hobbies, or seeking therapy allows you to manage stress, anxiety, and depression effectively. By nurturing your mental and spiritual health, you develop resilience and the ability to navigate life's challenges with a positive mindset.

To achieve this, you need to dig deep, and I'm going to trust you will actually do this. In life, you have many experiences. These experiences mold you into who you are. These can be good or bad. But they are not you. They are experiences.

I want you to take a moment to stop, meditate, and dig deep inside of you. *If you have not meditated before, download our app and start the free meditation practices.*

Get yourself in a comfortable position with a straight back. You want your body aligned. It's helpful to close your eyes.

Let all your thoughts fade away. Don't worry, they will come back later. Just breath. Notice your breath.

Allow your memory to float to whatever pops up. And allow it to come.

Feel it, remember it, and think about how you felt at that age, at that time in your life, knowing what you knew at that time. Allow yourself the experience of the emotion. This will allow it to be removed forever.

If another memory pops up, follow it. Does it lead to another memory from when you were younger? Keep allowing these experiences to come until you reach the youngest age you remember feeling this way. You are looking for a pattern. Something that feels like "this isn't right," "that's not fair," or "that's not how life is."

Keep experiencing until you find the root of the experience. Once there, consider the impossibilities and possibilities. Was it what you thought? How do you feel about it now? Here, you will find a root pattern from before the age of 7. This is a seed that was planted in your memory, which is now a part of your bio memory. You will find this pattern consistent with its logic in your life.

You can alter this a bit as you go. You can use a mirror if that helps and look into the mirror during this process. You can also write. You do you.

The goal is to find the patterns and release them. Allowing you to no longer continue the pattern and be free to live the abundant life you deserve. Don't rush this process. It can take a week to acclimate to it. But once you start, it's so powerful, and you own your own destiny! I practice this every morning and evening. It's amazing!

Relationships are important in life. There are countless studies on human interaction and types of relationships. Do you have healthy relationships? I'm talking about those people who respect you, love you, and support you. Allowing you the freedom to fully express your authentic self. If you look around and don't have this, then you need a relationship upgrade. We talked about this already. I'm just here to remind you of its importance. Attract individuals who respect and support you. This is nurturing for you and allows you to give and receive love from a place of abundance, enhancing the quality of our connections. This comes up a lot, especially when we lack boundaries or healthy social encounters.

I'd like to add that sometimes we outgrow people, or they outgrow us, and this is okay. People come in and out of our lives as the universe finds a reciprocal relationship between your two's development.

When you love and care for yourself, you become more attuned to your values, passions, and goals. This self-awareness empowers you to make choices aligned with your authentic self, leading to a sense of purpose and fulfillment. By prioritizing self-care and self-love, you embark on a journey of personal growth and self-actualization.

In order to fully embrace and own your self-love while not being disturbed by others' thoughts and actions, it is essential to establish a consistent self-care routine. Here's a step-by-step approach to incorporating self-care into your daily life:

Reflect on the areas of your life where you feel depleted or neglected. Identify activities or practices that bring you joy, relaxation, and a sense of inner peace.

Develop a structured plan that includes different aspects of self-care, such as physical, emotional, mental, and spiritual well-being. Set realistic goals and make a commitment to prioritize self-care regularly.

Carve out dedicated time each day or week for self-care activities. It may be as simple as taking a long bath, reading a book, or meditating. Ensure you protect this time and treat it as non-negotiable.

Learn to say no to tasks and commitments that do not align with your self-care needs. Communicate your boundaries with others and kindly assert your priorities.

Be gentle with yourself when setbacks occur or when it feels challenging to prioritize self-care. Remember that self-love is a journey, and every small step counts.

By following these steps and integrating self-care practices into your life, you'll cultivate a strong foundation of self-love and resilience. Remember, self-love is an ongoing process that requires patience and consistent effort. Cherish yourself, prioritize your well-being, and watch as your healthier lifestyle unfolds, leaving you less affected by the thoughts and actions of others. You deserve to embrace and own your self-love wholeheartedly!

Now that we understand the significance of self-care and self-love, let's take a look at a step-by-step checklist to help you incorporate self-care into your daily life and cultivate a strong foundation of self-love and resilience.

Checklist

1. **Assess the impact:** Consider how the decision will affect your mental, emotional, and physical well-being. Will it contribute to self-care and self-love, or will it compromise them?

2. **Reflect on priorities:** Evaluate if the decision aligns with your values, passions, and goals. Is it in line with your authentic self and your long-term growth and fulfillment?

3. **Consider long-term consequences:** Think about the potential consequences of the decision in the future. Will it lead to sustainable self-care and self-love, or will it hinder your progress?

4. **Seek support:** Reach out to individuals who understand the importance of self-care and self-love. Consult with mentors, friends, or professionals who can provide guidance and different perspectives.

5. **Set boundaries:** Determine if the decision respects and supports your boundaries. Will it allow you to prioritize your needs and protect your well-being?

6. **Practice self-compassion:** Be kind and understanding towards yourself during the decision-making process. Remember that self-love is a journey, and that setbacks and challenges are a natural part of it.

7. **Visualize the outcome:** Envision how the decision will contribute to your overall well-being and self-love. Will it bring you joy, peace, and growth?

8. **Take action:** Make a confident and intentional decision that prioritizes your self-care and self-love. Trust yourself and your ability to choose what is best for your well-being.

9. **Evaluate and adjust:** Continuously assess the impact of the decision on your self-care and self-love. Adjust your actions and choices accordingly to ensure they align with your evolving needs.

10. **Embrace self-love:** Celebrate and acknowledge yourself for making decisions that prioritize self-care and self-love. Embrace and own your self-love wholeheartedly throughout the decision-making process and beyond.

I like giving you stories and examples to help you understand more and maybe adapt more easily. I'd like to share Mary's story with you now.

Case Study: The Impact of Self-Care and Self-Love on Mary's Well-Being

Let's take a look at Mary, a 35-year-old woman who works as a highly successful executive at a demanding corporate job. She has always prioritized her career, often sacrificing her own well-being for professional success. However, after experiencing burnout and severe mental health issues, Mary realized the importance of self-care and self-love in achieving a healthier lifestyle.

Mary recognized that her mental and emotional well-being were crucial to her overall happiness. She started practicing mindfulness meditation for 20 minutes every morning. Through this practice, Mary learned to manage her stress, anxiety, and depression more effectively. Over time, she developed resilience and a positive mindset, allowing her to navigate work and personal challenges with ease.

Mary incorporated regular exercise and a balanced diet into her routine. She started her yoga practice and committed to working out each morning. She also started cooking nutritious meals at home and reduced her intake of processed foods. As a result, Mary noticed an increase in her energy levels, improved immune system, and a healthy body weight.

By prioritizing self-care and self-love, Mary established healthier relationships with herself and others. She learned to set boundaries, express her needs, and value her own well-being. As a result, Mary attracted supportive and respectful individuals into her life. She nurtured her relationships with her loved ones more effectively, resulting in deeper connections and improved communication.

Through self-care practices and self-love, Mary became more attuned to her values, passions, and goals. She realized that her true purpose was not solely focused on professional success but also on personal growth and fulfillment. Mary set aside time each week to pursue her hobbies, such as painting and writing. These activities allowed her to explore her creativity and passions, resulting in a greater sense of empowerment and self-actualization.

> Mary engaged in mindfulness meditation for 20 minutes every morning. She started a yoga practice and committed to morning yoga. Integrated with cooking nutritious meals at home and reducing processed food intake helped her start her day positively and with vitality.
>
> Mary also set boundaries and expressed her needs in relationships. While pursuing hobbies like painting and writing on a regular basis. All of this filled her with bliss and made each day something to look forward to.
>
> She was able to clearly see a decreased level of stress, anxiety, and depression. Her energy increased and her physical health improved. Mary's relationships changed as well. She enhanced relationships with loved ones, characterized by better communication and deeper connections. All this gave her a greater sense of empowerment, personal growth, and self-actualization.

Don't think this was easy. She had challenges along the way. Mary faced several challenges throughout her journey towards self-care and self-love. She initially struggled with guilt and self-judgment when prioritizing her own needs over work or other responsibilities. It was challenging for her to set boundaries and assert her priorities. Additionally, she experienced resistance from others who were accustomed to her always being available and constantly sacrificing her own well-being.

> In the end, Mary's ability to implement self-care was not selfish but necessary for overall well-being. By prioritizing self-love and self-care, she was required to set boundaries and assert Her priorities. Mary also realized the journey towards self-love is ongoing and requires patience and consistent effort. This is why it was so important for her to surround herself with individuals who understood and supported self-care, knowing it was crucial for success.

Overall, the impact of Mary's self-care and self-love journey has been transformative. She experienced significant improvements in her mental and emotional well-being, physical health, relationships, and personal growth. Mary became a stronger, more resilient, and fulfilled individual. By prioritizing self-care and self-love, Mary embraced her divine being and is less affected by the thoughts and actions of others.

After witnessing the transformative impact of Mary's journey towards self-care and self-love, it is important to highlight the common mistakes to avoid in order to achieve similar levels of well-being and fulfillment. By recognizing and addressing these mistakes, you can navigate your own self-care journey more effectively and experience positive changes in your mental, emotional, and physical health, relationships, and personal growth.

Based on all the things I dropped here, we all make mistakes. Here are some common ones most people make: neglecting their own needs, seeking validation from others, and failing to establish boundaries. These mistakes can be avoided by:

1. Assessing your own needs and prioritizing activities that bring you joy and inner peace.
2. Creating a structured self-care plan that includes different aspects of well-being.
3. Dedicate time for self-care activities and treat it as non-negotiable.
4. Establishing and communicating boundaries with others to prevent overcommitting.
5. Practicing self-compassion and being gentle with yourself when setbacks occur.
6. Seeking support from individuals who understand the importance of self-care and self-love.

We just went over a lot, so let's quickly review:

- **Get your priorities straight:** Prioritizing self-care and self-love is essential for achieving and maintaining a healthier lifestyle.

- **Putting yourself first:** Self-care promotes mental and emotional well-being, giving us the tools to navigate life's challenges with a positive mindset.

- **Connection to physical health:** Taking care of our physical health through self-care practices boosts our energy levels and prevents chronic illnesses.

- **Relationships matter:** Self-care and self-love enhance the quality of our relationships, attracting those who respect and support us.

- **Become authentic:** By prioritizing self-care and self-love, we empower ourselves to make choices aligned with our authentic selves, leading to personal growth and fulfillment.

It's your favorite part, digging in...

1. Identify what is holding you back from your self-care and self-love:

_____
_____
_____
_____

2. What will you commit to first for your physical health?

_____
_____
_____
_____

3. What will you commit to first for your mental health?

_____
_____
_____
_____

4. What will you commit to first for your spiritual health?

_____
_____
_____
_____

5. What does your self-care plan look like?

_____
_____
_____
_____

6. What does your self-love look like?

_____
_____
_____
_____

7. How will you implement these into your life? (Remember, ease into this for sustainable success.)

_____
_____
_____
_____

8. What are your thoughts and plans to improve your relationships?

_____

_____

_____

_____

Now that we've explored the power of self-care and self-love in nurturing a healthier lifestyle, we will delve into another vital aspect of well-being: how healthy boundaries can greatly enhance our mental and emotional health. Keep reading to discover the transformative impact of boundaries and learn practical ways to effortlessly incorporate this into your life.

Chapter 6

Setting Boundaries: Your Guide to Establishing Healthy Relationships and Protecting Your Well-Being

"Boundaries define who you are and what you stand for, so don't be afraid to set them and defend them fiercely."

- **unknown**

- Understand the concept of personal boundaries: Identify your boundaries so you can know when they need enforcing.
- Recognize your limits and needs: Learn how self-awareness and introspection support your boundaries.
- Communicate effectively: Practice expressing your needs and limits respectfully yet firmly, allowing others to understand and respect your boundaries.
- Communicate assertively: Gain clarity by using confident and assertive language to express your limits and expectations.
- Be consistent: Explore your boundary maintenance by enforcing consequences when they are crossed.

Let's be real. We all need better boundaries, especially in our society with the demands of achieving through our careers and the pressures we all face as we evolve. Boundaries are often pushed, and eventually, the lack of them becomes the norm. Setting boundaries and developing an action plan towards a healthier and happier lifestyle is not just a luxury, but a necessity. It's one of the major reasons we end up feeling so lost and hopeless. You are responsible to protect your mental, emotional, and physical well-being. By setting boundaries, you establish your expectations and limits for how others treat you, as well as how you treat yourself.

Boundaries empower you to create healthier relationships and eliminate toxic relationships. When you clearly define your limits, you reduce the chances of being taken advantage of or feeling overwhelmed. You gain control over your own life and decisions, promoting a sense of self-respect and self-worth.

But setting boundaries is just the first step. To truly make a positive change, you need to develop an action plan. This plan allows you to actively work towards implementing and maintaining those boundaries.

To be honest, I had such a terrible understanding of this myself. I didn't even realize I had no boundaries. Life taught me the hard way. If this is you, you get it. So many times, even though I didn't want to do something, I would because it seemed like the expectation would have some type of reward or relief. But that isn't true. I'll give you two quick personal examples.

Let's start off with work. In this area of my life, I was the only one working. So, my job was critical to me and the girls. Due to my own stress and needs, I allowed my schedule to be manipulated so much that I didn't even have a day off and worked 12-hour days. After a few months of this, it just became the expectation from my boss. I was burnt out and miserable after a few years of this. I ended up getting another job just to get a break. Many years later, I took a job that I thought was going to be great. The first night I was working at 9 pm, I was done. The next day, I said there was no way I would work that late again, and I quit. Work isn't my life. My life is my life's work (enriching lives, not companies who want my soul).

In my personal life, I was even worse. I was in so many relationships that took advantage of me that I eventually had to cut those people off and had decided for years to have no friends or intimate relationships because I just didn't have the energy to give anymore. I was happier on my own taking care of the girls.

My lack of boundaries was not my own discovery, by the way. It was a session with my counselor, who asked me what my boundaries were. After thinking for a hot minute, I said

I didn't really have any except if anyone were to physically harm me or my girls. This does make me laugh because now I have a whole list of them!

I was pretty lucky to get help in these areas as I got older. But now, I guard my boundaries like I would protect my own life. It's the essence of who I am, and I choose who I give my time to and how much I give them, and I know why I do it.

The first thing you must do is identify the areas of your life that require boundary setting. Is it in your personal relationships, work, or self-care? Make a list of the specific behaviors or actions that you find unacceptable or draining.

Next, create a strategy for each area. This seemed silly to me at first until I realized the patterns were repeating. Immediately that night, I made myself process what I would do if the said boundary was pushed or crossed. Consider what steps you need to take to communicate your boundaries clearly and assertively. Determine the consequences you're willing to enforce if those boundaries are crossed repeatedly.

Realizing boundary setting is an ongoing process, and it requires consistency and self-care. This might seem challenging at first. Surprisingly, it doesn't take much effort after you start practicing holding your boundaries and assessing how interactions make you feel. Regularly reassess your boundaries and adjust them as needed. Remember that it's okay to make changes along the way as you grow and learn more about what you need and deserve. Five years ago, I was not the same person I am today. I have different boundaries, and I am willing to lose everything for them.

Implementing an action plan has numerous benefits. It brings structure and clarity to your life. It reduces stress, anxiety, and resentment. It allows you to prioritize your needs and preserve your mental and emotional well-being. The action plan here is not a hard one. Meaning it's not something you really have to put all your effort into. It's as simple as following your list of boundaries and implementing the most critical ones first.

So, take charge. Set those boundaries, develop your action plan, and start creating the healthier and happier lifestyle you deserve. Remember, you have the power to create positive change in your life, and setting boundaries is a pivotal step toward achieving that.

Checklist

1. **Decide to prioritize self-care:** Recognize that setting boundaries is a form of self-care. Decide that your well-being is a top priority and that you deserve to protect your well-being.

2. **Identify your limits:** Take the time to understand your limits and what makes you feel comfortable or uncomfortable in different situations. This is being self-aware and present. Determine what behaviors or actions you find unacceptable or draining.

3. **Clearly communicate your boundaries:** Make the decision to assertively and directly communicate your boundaries to others. Decide to use confident and assertive language when expressing your limits, making it clear that they are non-negotiable.

4. **Always enforce consequences:** Establish the decision to enforce consequences when your boundaries are crossed once or repeatedly. Determine what actions you will take if someone continues to disrespect or violate your boundaries. Consistency in enforcing consequences is essential for maintaining boundaries effectively.

5. **Allow yourself flexibility to regularly reassess and adjust boundaries:** Recognize that your boundaries may evolve over time as you grow and change. Decide to regularly reassess and adjust your boundaries to

ensure they continue to align with your needs and values.

Making these decisions and sticking to them is crucial for setting healthy boundaries. Remember, you have the power to protect your well-being and create a fulfilling and balanced life by setting and maintaining boundaries that serve you.

You will thank yourself later for this chapter. For now, let's go over some other examples to really let this sink in.

Gina recognized that she was constantly overwhelmed and burnt out from taking on too many responsibilities. She set a boundary by communicating to her family that she needed designated time each evening to unwind and recharge. Now, she prioritizes self-care during that time, whether it's taking a bath, reading a book, or practicing meditation.

Mae had a high-stress job and realized that she was constantly being pulled in different directions at work, leading to increased stress and decreased productivity. She implemented a boundary by setting specific office hours and strictly adhering to them. She communicated to her colleagues that after a certain time, she would not be available unless it was an urgent matter. By doing so, she regained control over her time and improved her work-life balance.

Sarah, a young adult setting boundaries with her parents, found that her parents often crossed boundaries when it came to her personal decisions and independence. She made the decision to have an open and honest conversation with them, expressing her need for autonomy and privacy. By clearly communicating her boundaries and expectations, she established a healthier and more respectful dynamic with her parents.

Deanna was a recovering addict, and she recognized that toxic relationships were hindering her recovery. She made the courageous decision to cut ties with friends who enabled her addictive behaviors and set boundaries regarding her sobriety. She surrounded herself with a supportive network of individuals who respected her boundaries and encouraged her healthy choices.

Lisa's life had completely been taken over by caring for her elderly parents. Caregiving left her little time for her own needs and well-being. She set boundaries by delegating certain responsibilities to other family members and hiring outside help. She established clear guidelines for her availability and made self-care a non-negotiable priority. By doing so, she regained a sense of balance and restored her own sense of self.

These individuals exemplify the power of setting healthy boundaries in different aspects of life to protect their well-being, maintain balance, and cultivate healthier relationships. All of them love the enjoyable time they now have with their friends and loved ones. They are rejuvenated and have more energy for their passions.

Depending on the boundaries and how long you have let them slide, this can be challenging. If you thought at all from the above examples these people were selfish, lazy, or any other negative idea, you need this book to save your life. Get that programming out of your head. Look inside yourself and your longings. What are you missing? Not in the thought, but what are you missing in your life? This is a big mistake.

Let me share a few more I have seen. Avoiding these mistakes will help you establish and maintain healthy boundaries effectively. Here's what to watch out for:

1. Being unclear or ambiguous: One mistake is failing to clearly articulate your boundaries to others. Vague or unclear boundaries can lead to confusion and misunderstandings. Be specific and direct when expressing your limits, making sure that others understand your expectations.

2. People-pleasing tendencies: Many women struggle with the fear of disappointing others, which can result in compromising or even sacrificing their own boundaries. Remember, setting boundaries is

necessary for your well-being, so prioritize your needs instead of constantly trying to please others.

3. Inconsistent enforcement: Another common mistake is not following through on consequences when boundaries are crossed. Consistency is key to creating and maintaining healthy boundaries. If you fail to enforce consequences, others may not take your boundaries seriously, leading to their repeated violation. It's always amazing the lack of self-awareness there is out in the world. Some people just genuinely have no clue they are pushing boundaries.

4. Guilt or self-doubt: People often feel guilty or doubt their decision to set boundaries, especially when confronted with pushback from others. It's essential to recognize that setting boundaries is not selfish but an act of self-care and self-respect. Maintain confidence in your choices, and don't let guilt derail your boundary-setting efforts.

5. Neglecting self-care: Lastly, people sometimes forget to prioritize their own well-being while focusing on establishing boundaries with others. Remember that self-care is crucial for maintaining your well-being. Incorporate self-care activities into your routine to ensure you have the energy and resilience to maintain your boundaries effectively.

Learning from these mistakes and taking steps to avoid them will strengthen your ability to set and maintain healthy personal boundaries. You can create better relationships, protect your well-being, and lead a more balanced and fulfilling life.

Work through the follow-on questions to help you better understand your boundaries. Allow the answers to be your guide. Take time to understand you. Maybe reflect on the answers you gave in prior chapters to help guide you through these. You'll be empowered to protect your well-being, prioritize your needs, and cultivate healthier relationships in your life by considering these questions and thoughtfully planning your personal boundaries.

Get your shovel (pen), and let's dig in:

1. What are my core values and beliefs that I want to protect and honor through my boundaries?

_____
_____
_____
_____

2. What are the specific behaviors or actions from others that make me uncomfortable or violate my sense of well-being?

_____
_____
_____
_____

3. In what areas of my life do I consistently feel overwhelmed, drained, or taken advantage of?

_____
_____
_____
_____

4. What are my non-negotiable needs for self-care, personal time, and space to recharge?

_____

_____

_____

_____

5. How can I effectively assert my boundaries and communicate them to others in a clear and respectful manner?

_____

_____

_____

_____

6. Who are the individuals in my life from whom I need to establish firm boundaries, and what are the specific limits I want to set with them?

_____

_____

_____

_____

7. What are the consequences I am willing to enforce if my boundaries are repeatedly crossed?

_____

_____

_____

_____

8. Are there any patterns or habits that I need to recognize and address within myself to establish healthier boundaries?

_____

_____

_____

_____

9. How can I ensure consistency in maintaining my boundaries and not compromising them during challenging situations?

_____

_____

_____

_____

10. What support systems or resources can I access to help me establish and reinforce my personal boundaries effectively?

_____
_____
_____
_____

Now that we've dug deep into our boundaries and questioned everything… just kidding…maybe; let's shift to ripping off the next band-aid. Our freedom from breaking our destructive habits, behaviors, or addictions that might be hindering our progress. Yes, we are going here next.

Keep in mind that I have gone through all these steps. Just over a decade, it took me. And with a lot of patient people, I eventually figured it out. Once I realized the secret sauce, I started helping others do this quickly and effectively.

I know this is hard. I know sometimes it hurts. I know you set the book down and breathe. I also know you are tired. Tired of the life you have been living and ready for change. Effective, real change!

So, keep going! You are doing this! You are a beautiful soul who deserves to be happy. It's your divine right to live a life of bliss and fulfill your potential! Now, get back to work!

Chapter 7

Breaking Chains, Embracing Freedom: Overcoming Destructive Habits for Personal Progress

"The only person you are destined to become is the person you decide to be."

- Ralph Waldo Emerson

- Explore the root causes: Uncover the hidden emotions and triggers behind destructive habits, behaviors, or addictions, clearing the path for transformation.
- Replace negativity with positivity: Discover fulfilling activities that bring you joy and serve as healthy outlets for stress and emotions.
- Build a supportive network: Surround yourself with like-minded individuals who understand your journey and can offer guidance and encouragement.
- Establish a stable routine: Create a structured daily routine that promotes predictability and reduces the risk of falling back into destructive habits.

- Practice self-care and self-compassion: Treat yourself with kindness and celebrate the small victories, nurturing your journey towards a better future.
-

Breaking free from destructive habits, behaviors, or addictions is clearly a challenging journey, but we all have them, and we must create a well-structured approach and commitment to achieve freedom from them. To successfully overcome hindrances to progress, you need to address the root causes, develop alternative coping mechanisms, and create a stable environment to support your transformation. Allow me to guide you through the step-by-step process.

It's private here. You are just in your own head and self-talk. Take a moment and be honest with yourself. Recognize and confront the habits: The first essential step is to identify and acknowledge the destructive habits, behaviors or addictions that are impeding your progress. This involves honest self-reflection and a willingness to confront the negative patterns in your life. It is helpful to meditate and keep a journal, documenting instances when these habits or addictions surface, along with associated triggers and emotions. This level of detail will provide a foundation for you to move forward.

Once you are done, review Chapter 5's practice, where we dug in, to understand the root patterns in our life. This will help you understand the underlying emotions and triggers: Destructive habits often arise as coping mechanisms for deeper feelings. Take the time to explore and understand the emotions and triggers that contribute to these habits. It may be beneficial to seek the assistance of a therapist or counselor who can guide you through this process or to join our program to get you unstuck. By gaining clarity on the underlying causes, you can proactively address them, paving the way for sustainable change.

Often, professionals will suggest replacing destructive habits with positive alternatives. You can do this method. I personally gained the most benefit for lasting results through the pattern-digging process. But if you decide to go with the replacement method, you do you.

Let's look at the replacement method first. This involves you replacing them with healthier alternatives that serve as productive outlets for emotions and stress. Engage in activities that bring you joy, spark creativity, or provide a sense of fulfillment. This could include hobbies, exercise, meditation, or connecting with supportive friends and family members. Experiment with different activities and find what resonates with you.

We talked about this already, and I can't stress it enough. You need support! Establishing a support system and building a stable environment is crucial for breaking free from destructive habits and addictions. Surround yourself with individuals who support your journey towards positive change. Seek out support groups, join online communities, or engage in therapy sessions to connect with like-minded individuals who have overcome similar challenges. Lean on this support system during times of struggle and celebrate your progress with them.

Developing a routine and structure should be no surprise at this point. It is the key to creating your true potential. A stable environment is needed to support your routine and structure in your daily life. Establishing specific times for sleep, meals, exercise, work/study, and leisure activities helps create a sense of predictability and stability. Having a well-structured routine reduces the likelihood of falling back into destructive habits, behaviors, or addictions, as every aspect of your life now follows a healthier pattern. Keep it simple; remove the access to the behavior, habit, or addiction.

Practice self-care and self-compassion: Yep, it's this subject again. Breaking free from our behaviors is a journey that requires perseverance and self-compassion. Treat yourself with kindness and patience throughout this process. Engage in regular self-care activities such as the options we have discussed already. Celebrate small milestones and recognize your progress, no matter how small.

I want to touch on self-compassion for a second. This bit we have consistently overlooked in society. We look for big wins or something we believe others will recognize as milestones. The truth is this is all about you and your journey. So, if you have been waking up at 6 a.m. and have a goal to wake up at 4 a.m. every day, you wake up a little earlier. Maybe it's just 5 minutes earlier. Who cares? You did it! You woke up earlier. Own this! Each day, you wake up just a bit earlier, and before you know it, you are waking up on time!

Breaking free from our behaviors is a process. Everything in this book is a process. If you are skimming through it, you are doing yourself a massive injustice. Each of these is important. They require time, effort, and a commitment to self-improvement. By following these steps and implementing them consistently, you can gradually overcome the hurdles that hinder your progress. Trust in yourself and the process, and remember that change is possible when approached with a thorough and supportive mindset.

Now that we have explored the step-by-step process of breaking free from destructive habits and addictions, let's dive deeper into the practical implementation of these steps with the help of the checklist I have created.

Checklist

1. **First Recognize:** Recognize and acknowledge destructive habits, behaviors, or addictions.
2. **Be honest:** Engage in honest self-reflection and confront negative patterns.
3. **Common support:** Build a support system of like-minded individuals who have overcome similar challenges.
4. **Get support:** Join support groups or online communities, or engage in therapy sessions for additional support.
5. **Create routine:** Establish a routine and structure in your daily life.
6. **Love yourself:** Practice self-care and self-compassion throughout the recovery process.
7. **Progress in the right direction counts:** Celebrate small milestones and recognize your progress, no matter how small.

Now, let's explore some examples that cognize how these steps can be implemented in real-life situations.

Monica realizes that her excessive use of social media is hindering her productivity and overall well-being. She takes the first step by recognizing and acknowledging this destructive habit. She started keeping a journal, documenting when and why she feels the need to constantly check her notifications and posts.

Jennifer has been struggling with alcohol addiction for years. After hitting rock bottom, she decides to confront her habit and seek help. She starts attending therapy sessions where she explores and understands the underlying emotions and triggers that lead to his alcohol abuse.

Emma wants to break free from her habit of stress-eating. She realizes that she turns to unhealthy foods as a coping mechanism for her anxiety. Rather than reaching for junk food, she starts replacing this habit with alternative coping mechanisms such as going for a walk, doing yoga, or journaling her thoughts and emotions.

Michelle knows that a stable environment is crucial for overcoming her addiction to gambling. She cuts ties with friends who enable his behavior and surrounds herself with supportive individuals. She also joins a support group where she meets others who have successfully overcome their gambling problems, providing her with encouragement and guidance.

Maria understands the importance of structure in her journey to break free from her habit of procrastination. She creates a routine where she sets specific times for studying, breaks, and leisure activities. By following this structure, she reduces the likelihood of falling into old patterns of avoiding responsibilities.

Daniel practices self-care and self-compassion as she works to overcome her addiction to smoking. She replaces smoking breaks with healthier activities such as pattern digging. She celebrates every smoke-free day and acknowledges her progress, no matter how small it may seem.

These can all be applied to other behaviors you just don't want to do anymore. For example, I have a student who discovered she needed to change her diet due to her own decision to eat a religious diet. This was very difficult for her because she was the only one in her household who was practicing, and she loved to eat the other foods. Foodies was an understatement in this family. But she went through this process and quickly realized her core value of living this life was more important than the food she was eating. So, she easily adjusted after going through the questions. The behavior just stopped.

These examples illustrate how different individuals can apply the steps mentioned in the original answer to break free from destructive habits, behaviors, or addictions. Each person's journey is unique, but the approach of addressing root causes, developing alternative coping mechanisms, digging into patterns, and creating a stable environment remains consistent.

Now that we have explored these examples, let's take a closer look at a case study that demonstrates how an individual applied these steps to overcome a destructive habit.

Case Study: Overcoming Substance Abuse

Julie is a 35-year-old woman who has been struggling with substance abuse for the past 10 years. Her addiction to alcohol and drugs has greatly hindered her personal and professional growth, causing strained relationships and financial instability. Recognizing the destructive nature of her habits, Julie decides to embark on a journey to break free and transform her life.

Julie realizes that her substance abuse has been a major hindrance in her life and is determined to overcome it. She starts by maintaining a journal, noting down instances when he succumbs to her addiction and the triggers and emotions associated with each episode. This helps her gain a deeper understanding of her destructive habits.

Julie seeks the assistance of a therapist who helps her explore the underlying emotions and triggers fueling her substance abuse. Through therapy sessions, she identifies that her addiction is a coping mechanism for unresolved trauma and anxiety. This self-reflection helps Julie develop a clearer understanding of her root causes.

To address the emotional issues that drive her addiction, Julie decides to adopt alternative coping mechanisms. She starts exercising regularly, which helps her channel her stress and boosts her mood. Additionally, she takes up painting as a creative outlet and participates in support group meetings where she finds solace and encouragement from others who understand her struggle.

Julie realizes the importance of building a stable environment to break free from her destructive habits. She joins a local support group that provides her with a supportive community of people who have overcome similar challenges. The constant encouragement, understanding, and accountability from these individuals significantly contribute to Julie's progress.

To maintain stability in her life, Julie creates a structured routine. She establishes specific times for sleep, meals, exercise, work, and leisure activities. By adhering to this routine, Julie reduces the risk of falling back into destructive habits, as she now has healthier patterns in her daily life.

Throughout her journey, Julie practices self-care and self-compassion. She engages in regular mindfulness exercises, journaling, and taking time for relaxing activities. By celebrating small milestones and recognizing her progress, Julie reinforces her commitment to the process and nurtures a positive mindset.

After committing to this well-structured approach, Julie experiences significant improvements in various aspects of her life. She successfully completed a detox program and remained sober for six months. Julie is now employed in a stable job and has restored her relationships with family and friends. She no longer relies on substances to cope with stress and has developed healthy mechanisms to deal with emotions.

Julie encountered several challenges along the way, including cravings, withdrawal symptoms, and moments of self-doubt. However, with the support of her therapist, the guidance of the support group, and her own determination, she was able to overcome these obstacles.

Julie learned that confronting her destructive habits head-on and seeking professional help were crucial in her journey to overcome addiction. She also realized the importance of a stable support system and the power of adopting healthy coping mechanisms. Through self-reflection and self-compassion, she discovered that change is possible and achievable with commitment and perseverance.

Julie's transformation from a person trapped in destructive habits to someone leading a fulfilling life exemplifies the powerful impact of the step-by-step process discussed in the article. By addressing the root causes, developing alternative coping mechanisms, creating a stable environment, and practicing self-care, Julie successfully broke free from her destructive behavior. Her journey showcases the immense potential for positive change when individuals are willing to commit to self-improvement.

Having examined Julie's journey of overcoming substance abuse, we can now turn our attention to a list of mistakes to avoid to achieve success in similar endeavors. These mistakes, when avoided, can greatly enhance the chances of breaking free from destructive habits and creating a healthier and more fulfilling life.

I've learned one mistake that most people make in breaking free from destructive habits, behaviors, or addictions is not addressing the root causes of their habits. It is important to recognize and confront the habits, as well as understand the underlying patterns that contribute to them. This can be achieved through honest self-reflection, digging deep into our patterns, and seeking assistance.

Additionally, not establishing a support system can hinder progress. Building a stable environment and surrounding yourself with individuals who support your journey towards positive change is crucial. This can be done by joining support groups, engaging in therapy sessions, or connecting with like-minded individuals who have overcome similar challenges.

Another mistake is not developing a routine and structure in daily life. Having specific times for sleep, meals, exercise, work/study, and leisure activities helps create a sense of predictability and stability. This reduces the likelihood of falling back into destructive habits.

Let's not forget our self-care and self-compassion; it's a common area overlooked. Breaking free from destructive habits requires perseverance and treating yourself with kindness and patience. Regular self-care activities, such as practicing mindfulness, journaling, taking relaxing baths, or engaging in hobbies, should be incorporated. It is important to celebrate small milestones and recognize progress, no matter how small.

In order to avoid these mistakes, you should focus on addressing the root causes, replacing destructive habits with positive alternatives, establishing a support system, developing a routine and structure, and practicing self-care and self-compassion. By following these steps consistently, you can overcome the obstacles that hinder their progress.

This was a lot to cover. Let's recap real quick:

- **Recognize and confront destructive habits:** Take an honest look at the habits that are holding you back and be willing to confront them head-on.
- **Understand the underlying emotions:** Explore the deeper emotional issues that contribute to your

destructive habits, seek help if needed, and gain clarity to proactively address them.

- **Replace destructive habits with positive alternatives:** Find productive outlets for your emotions and stress by engaging in activities that bring you joy, creativity, or fulfillment.

- **Establish a support system:** Surround yourself with supportive individuals who understand your journey and seek out support groups or therapy sessions to connect with like-minded individuals.

- **Develop a routine and structure:** Create a stable environment by establishing a routine that includes specific times for sleep, meals, exercise, work/study, and leisure activities.

- **Practice self-care and self-compassion:** Be kind and patient with yourself throughout the process, engage in regular self-care activities, and celebrate your progress, no matter how small. Trust in yourself and the process, knowing that change is possible with a thorough and supportive mindset.

With that, let's dig:

1. Identify the habits, behaviors, and addictions you have that you want to resolve now:

_____
_____
_____
_____

2. Take the time now to walk through the process of digging into your patterns. You can go back to Chapter 5 and follow the instructions there.

_____
_____
_____
_____

3. What did you discover as your pattern?

_____
_____
_____
_____

4. Do you feel you got to the ROOT of it?

_____
_____
_____
_____

5. What have you replaced the time you spent in these areas with?

_____
_____
_____
_____

6. Identify your support system to continue to stick to your new lifestyle. Who are they? How will they help you?

_____
_____
_____
_____

7. What have you established as your new routine?

_____
_____
_____
_____

8. Where did you identify self-compassion gaps?

_____
_____
_____
_____

9. What are some small milestones you can celebrate?

_____
_____
_____
_____

10. Do you trust yourself to keep to this?

_____
_____
_____
_____

Now that we have explored strategies to break free from destructive habits, it's time to delve into a new challenge that many face - feeling lost or disconnected from their purpose in life. Don't worry; you're not alone in this journey, and the advice shared in the following chapter will provide valuable insights to guide you back on track.

Chapter 8

Rediscovering Your True Path: Guidance for Reconnecting with Your Purpose in Life

"Your purpose in life is to find your purpose and give your whole heart and soul to it."

- Buddha

- Discover your true happiness: Learn how to navigate the challenging experience of feeling lost or disconnected from your purpose in life.
- Uncover your passions: Explore activities and hobbies that bring you joy and excitement, and use them as clues to finding your purpose.
- Find inspiration from others: Surround yourself with mentors, books, podcasts, and other sources that can guide and inspire you on your journey to discovering your purpose.
- Embrace the journey of personal growth: Understand that finding your purpose is a voyage of self-discovery and growth. Embrace challenges and setbacks as valuable lessons that bring you closer to your purpose.

- Take action toward your purpose: identify your real desires and create a plan to achieve them. Break down your desires into actionable steps that you can consistently take, and start building momentum toward finding your purpose.

Let's acknowledge the feeling of being lost or disconnected from one's purpose in life. It can be an incredibly challenging and disheartening experience. At some point in your life, you have probably asked yourself what your purpose is. May that be back in school when they asked what you wanted to be when you grow up, or you find yourself lost in the noise of society and one day realize you are lost. But please understand that you are not alone on this journey. Many people have faced similar struggles and have managed to rediscover their purpose, finding fulfillment and joy in the process.

Finding your purpose is your divine right and why you are here! Living a life of purpose IS what brings you to your full potential! Reality is not reality. Our society is not reality. Our bodies are not reality. Our reality is what we create, and the infinite is possible. All choices are yours, including reaching your true full potential.

This is a phase. Remember that. To guide you through this difficult phase, I would offer the following advice.

I have a theory about society. When we join the masses and work in the machine of society, with all the noise, we are slowly and sometimes bluntly denied our own time and this time to reflect. If we put ourselves first instead of the machine, we are failing, according to society, and we are programmed to think we are not successful. This couldn't be further from the truth. In truth, you must take the time to explore your own thoughts, emotions, and desires. Engage in introspection and ask yourself meaningful questions such as, "What brings me true happiness?" or "What are my core values and beliefs?" This process of self-reflection will help you gain insights into your innermost desires and provide clues to your purpose.

Explore various spiritual and philosophical traditions that resonate with you. Read books, attend lectures, or join discussion groups to understand different perspectives on life's purpose and the nature of existence. This alone will be very eye-opening for you. The similarities and the massive differences in each are amazing. Find something that works for you. I usually ask my students what their belief system is. It always amazes me that many don't know. They were brought up one way but didn't resonate with it for one reason or another. When you don't read the human interpretation of a belief but the authentic findings, often you will find the deep connection with these traditions and practices to be way more fulfilling and a place to bloom into bliss. Do your work and study. Find what works for you. When your soul lights up, you have found the right one for you.

You can also outgrow this. So don't feel stuck. You might be vibing with one practice and find later you don't have the same fulfillment. Spirituality is a practice and journey all of its own. As I shared before, I have practiced and studied many different beliefs. That's probably why I'm open to whatever anyone believes in. It's the interpretation and your experience that matters.

In my experience, finding inspiration has been hard for some people. Inspiration isn't always passive. Sure, you can surround yourself with sources of inspiration that resonate with you, like books, podcasts, or even mentors who have successfully found their purpose. But I would also add it can be active. Sometimes, I find inspiration in creating or doing. I'll paint a wall, write, weld. I find inspiration in doing things. I have learned from many mentors, though I have a vivacious appetite for learning. You can learn a lot from others. Stay open-minded and receptive to new ideas and perspectives.

Here's an option: get with a good Astrologer. They can pull your chart and give you this clarity. They will be able to identify areas of focus and how you might achieve this through the gifts you brought with you into this world. You will learn a lot about yourself. It can give you great peace of mind and a path to build around.

Understand that the journey towards finding your purpose is not one with a fixed destination or a linear path. It is a voyage of personal growth and self-discovery. Embrace the challenges and setbacks, as they often hold valuable lessons. At least you will know what you don't like and doesn't inspire you. It's like jokes; sometimes, they are hilarious, and other times, all you can do is give a courtesy laugh. You can always go back to the digging practice in Chapter 5 to help you understand yourself more. Cultivate a growth mindset, knowing that every experience contributes to your overall development and brings you closer to your purpose.

Don't overlook this part! Most of my students, regardless of the program they join when they find us, come to this place. They realize they have more to offer. They have dreams and desires to explore. Spirit is here to help you through. Incorporate spiritual practices that resonate with you into your daily life. This could include meditation, prayer, yoga, or any other rituals that help you connect with your higher self or divine power.

Pay attention to your inner voice or intuition. Trust your instincts and let them guide you towards a path of self-discovery and purpose.

Once you have gained some clarity, it is crucial to take action towards manifesting your purpose in your everyday life. Start by setting realistic goals and creating a plan to achieve them. Break down these goals into smaller, actionable steps that you can take consistently. By taking action, you will begin to build momentum towards finding your purpose.

Remember, finding your purpose is a deeply personal and unique journey. There is no one-size-fits-all approach, and it may take time and patience to fully understand and embrace your purpose. Trust in the process, have faith in yourself and stay committed to your personal growth. You are capable of discovering your purpose and leading a life filled with meaning and fulfillment.

Now that you have read the article and gained insights on how to find your purpose, I have created a checklist that will help you navigate through this journey with more clarity and direction.

Checklist

1. **Self-Reflection:**

    - Take time to explore your thoughts, emotions, and desires.
    - Ask meaningful questions to gain insights into your innermost desires.

- What brings you true happiness?
- What are your core values and beliefs?

2. **Explore Your Passions:**

    - Engage in activities or hobbies that excite you or bring you joy.
    - Follow your curiosity and fully immerse yourself in these activities.
    - Arts, sports, writing, volunteering, etc.
    - Uncover aspects of yourself and potential paths towards your purpose.

3. **Seek Inspiration:**

    - Surround yourself with sources of inspiration that resonate with you.
    - Books, podcasts, mentors who have found their purpose.
    - Learn from others who have overcome similar challenges.
    - Stay open-minded and receptive to new ideas.

4. **Embrace growth:**

    - Understand that the journey is not linear or fixed.
    - Embrace challenges and setbacks as valuable lessons.
    - Cultivate a growth mindset.
    - Every experience contributes to your overall development.

5. **Take Action:**

    - Gain clarity through self-reflection and exploration.
    - Set realistic goals and create a plan to achieve them.
    - Break down goals into smaller, actionable steps.
    - Take consistent action to build momentum.

6. **Remember:**

    - Finding your purpose is a personal and unique journey.
    - It may take time and patience.
    - Trust in the process and have faith in yourself.
    - Stay committed to personal growth and self-discovery.
    - You are capable of discovering your purpose and leading a meaningful life.

Now, let's look at this from what others have done.

Juanita, a recent college graduate, feels lost and unsure of what she wants to do with her life. She begins the process of self-reflection by journaling and reflecting on her past experiences. Through this introspection, she realizes that she has always enjoyed helping others and feels a sense of fulfillment when volunteering at her local homeless shelter. This leads her to explore potential careers in social work and nonprofit organizations, aligning with her values and passion for making a difference.

Jamie has been working in the corporate world for several years, but she feels unfulfilled and disconnected from her purpose. She decided to take up painting as a hobby, something she loved as a child but hadn't pursued in years. As she immerses herself in painting, she rediscovers the joy and creativity it brings her. Inspired by her newfound passion, she started attending art classes and eventually transitioned to a career as a professional artist, finding purpose and fulfillment in expressing herself through her art.

Emma, a college student, feels stuck and unsure of her future. She starts seeking inspiration by reading books and listening to podcasts about personal development and finding one's purpose. One book she comes across resonates deeply with her, detailing the journey of a successful entrepreneur who started her own business aligned with her passion for environmental sustainability. Inspired by this story, Emma starts researching and exploring environmental initiatives she can get involved in, eventually leading her to start her own eco-friendly business and find purpose in making a positive impact on the planet.

Dani is faced with a major setback in her career when she is unexpectedly laid off. Initially discouraged, she decides to embrace the challenge as an opportunity for growth and self-discovery. She takes the time to reflect on her skills and passions, realizing that she has always been interested in technology and problem-solving. Using the setback as motivation, she starts learning programming languages and eventually lands a job in the tech industry, rediscovering her purpose in building innovative solutions that improve people's lives.

Lily, a stay-at-home mom, feels a sense of emptiness and wants to find her purpose beyond her role as a mother. She starts by exploring her passions and realizes that she has always loved writing. She starts a blog to share her experiences and insights about motherhood and soon discovers a community of like-minded individuals who resonate with her words. Encouraged by the positive feedback, Lily starts writing a book and eventually becomes a published author, finding purpose in inspiring and connecting with others through her writing.

These examples illustrate how individuals from various backgrounds and life stages can navigate the journey of finding their purpose. Through self-reflection, exploration of passions, seeking inspiration, embracing growth, and taking action, each person is able to rediscover their purpose and create a fulfilling and meaningful life.

Let's unpack a case study that shines some light on the transformative power of finding purpose through self-reflection, exploration, and taking action.

Case Study: Rediscovering Purpose Through Self-Reflection and Action

Meadow, a 35-year-old professional, had been feeling disconnected from her purpose in life. She had been working in the finance industry for over a decade but had been feeling unfulfilled and unsatisfied with her career. Meadow decided to embark on a journey of self-discovery to reconnect with her spiritual connection and find a sense of purpose in her life.

Meadow started by dedicating time to self-reflection. She engaged in introspection, exploring her thoughts, emotions, and desires. She asked herself meaningful questions about her values, beliefs, and what brings her true happiness.

Meadow recognized the importance of exploring her passions and interests. She experimented with various activities and hobbies, such as painting, hiking, and volunteering. Through this exploration, she discovered a deep passion for environmental conservation and helping others.

To stay motivated and inspired, Meadow surrounded herself with sources of inspiration. She read books and listened to podcasts that shared stories of individuals who had overcome similar challenges and found their purpose. She also sought guidance from mentors who had successfully aligned their lives with their purpose.

Meadow embraced the challenges and setbacks she encountered throughout her journey. She understood that personal growth and self-discovery are not linear processes. Each setback provided an opportunity for learning and gaining valuable insights. Meadow cultivated a growth mindset, viewing every experience as contributing to her overall development.

After gaining clarity through self-reflection and exploration, Meadow took action towards manifesting her purpose. She set realistic goals and created a plan to achieve them. She started by volunteering for environmental organizations and taking courses related to sustainability. Meadow also began networking with professionals in the environmental field to expand her knowledge and potential opportunities.

Through her journey, Meadow experienced significant personal growth and measurable outcomes. She developed a deep passion for environmental conservation and sustainability. Meadow successfully transitioned from her finance career to a role as a sustainability manager in a nonprofit organization. She witnessed the positive impact she was making through her work, which further fueled her sense of purpose and fulfillment.

Meadow encountered several challenges along the way. She faced self-doubt and fear of leaving her stable finance job.

She also struggled with external pressures and societal expectations. Additionally, she had to overcome the hurdles of acquiring new skills and knowledge in a different field. However, Meadow's determination and commitment to her purpose allowed her to overcome these challenges.

Through this journey, Meadow learned several valuable lessons. She discovered the importance of self-reflection and exploration in uncovering her purpose. She realized that embracing challenges and setbacks was crucial for personal growth. It also taught her that taking consistent action, no matter how small, was essential for progress. Additionally, Meadow understood the significance of seeking inspiration from others who have successfully found their purpose.

Meadow's journey of rediscovering her purpose had a profound impact on her spiritual connection. By aligning his life with his values and passions, he developed a deep sense of fulfillment and a profound connection to something greater than herself. Meadow felt a newfound spiritual connection to nature and the environment, as she saw her work as an act of service to the planet and future generations.

Meadow's case study exemplifies the key information and points discussed. Through self-reflection, exploration of passions, seeking inspiration, embracing growth, and taking action, she rediscovered her purpose and achieved measurable outcomes. Despite the challenges faced, Meadow's journey had a positive impact on her spiritual connection, leading to a life filled with meaning and fulfillment.

Now that we have examined Meadow's inspiring case study of rediscovering purpose through self-reflection and action, let's take a closer look at some common mistakes to avoid when embarking on a similar journey.

- Not taking the time for self-reflection: Many people neglect to allocate time for introspection and self-exploration. This can prevent them from gaining insights into their true desires and purpose in life. Avoid this mistake by actively engaging in self-reflection and asking yourself meaningful questions, which, of course, we are going to get started here at the end of the chapter.

- Failing to explore passions and interests: Some individuals overlook the importance of exploring their passions and interests. By not actively engaging in activities that bring joy and excitement, they miss opportunities to uncover aspects of themselves and potential paths towards their purpose. Avoid this mistake by pursuing activities that genuinely excite you and allow for self-discovery.

- Neglecting to seek inspiration: Many people fail to surround themselves with sources of inspiration that resonate with them. This can limit their growth and hinder their journey towards finding their purpose. Avoid this mistake by seeking out inspiring books, podcasts, or mentors who have successfully found their purpose.

- Resisting growth and setbacks: Some individuals struggle with embracing challenges and setbacks, viewing them as deterrents rather than opportunities for growth. It is important to cultivate a growth mindset and understand that these challenges contribute to personal development. Avoid this mistake by embracing the challenges and setbacks, learning from them, and seeing them as stepping stones toward your purpose.

- Not taking action: One of the biggest mistakes is not taking action towards manifesting one's purpose in daily life. Without tangible steps and goals, it is difficult to make progress. Avoid this mistake by setting realistic goals and creating a plan to achieve them. Break down these goals into manageable steps that can be taken consistently.

To avoid these mistakes, it is essential to prioritize self-reflection, explore passions, seek inspiration, embrace growth, and take action. Remember that finding your purpose is a unique and personal journey that requires time, patience, and commitment to personal growth. Trust in yourself and the process, and you will be capable of discovering your purpose and leading a fulfilling life.

To avoid these common mistakes and to align yourself with your true purpose, it is essential to prioritize self-reflection, explore passions, seek inspiration, embrace growth, and take action. However, there is one piece of advice that stands above the rest and encompasses all of these elements.

Embrace your journey, trust in your own path, and cultivate a sense of gratitude for the present moment. Let go of judgment, comparison, and the need for external validation, and instead, seek solace in daily practices such as meditation, prayer, or connecting with nature. Remember, your journey is unique to you, and embracing this authenticity will lead to fulfillment and a deeper connection with yourself and the world around you.

Now remember:

- You are not alone in feeling lost or disconnected from your purpose in life.
- Self-reflection can provide insights into your desires and lead you toward your purpose.
- Explore your passions and interests to uncover potential paths towards your purpose.
- Seek a deeper understanding of life through spiritual practices and traditions.
- Surround yourself with sources of inspiration and learn from others who have found their purpose.
- Embrace challenges and setbacks as opportunities for growth and take action to manifest your purpose in everyday life.

It's that time…Let's dig in.

1. What brings you joy and fulfillment?

_____
_____
_____
_____

2. How do you define success?

_____
_____
_____
_____

3. What are your core values?

_____
_____
_____
_____

4. How can you enrich others' lives through your contributions?

_____
_____
_____
_____

5. What makes you feel connected to something greater than yourself?

_____
_____
_____
_____

6. What legacy do you want to leave?

_____
_____
_____
_____

As we explore ways to find our purpose in life, it's important to remember that identifying our desires and developing an action plan can be the key to unlocking a healthier and happier lifestyle that aligns with our true calling. Keep reading as we dive into the significance of our desires and discover practical steps to cultivate a life of fulfillment.

Chapter 9

The Path to a Healthier and Happier Life: Setting Achievable Goals and Creating an Action Plan

"The only limit to our realization of tomorrow will be our doubts of today."

- Franklin D. Roosevelt

- Discover the secret to creating a healthier and happier lifestyle by identifying your desires and a well-thought-out action plan.
- Supercharge your motivation and self-belief by acting on your desires that are meaningful.
- Unlock your full potential by using a structured action plan that breaks down your journey into manageable steps.
- Learn how to overcome obstacles and stay on track towards your desired outcomes with a comprehensive action plan.
- Experience personal growth and fulfillment by staying accountable to yourself and celebrating milestones along the way.

We all have desires. Creating a realistic action plan for obtaining yours makes them a reality. I would also add that believing in yourself and your ability to obtain this is the secret sauce. And let's be clear here. Goals are our desires. So, when you see the word goal. Don't get hung up on the decades of sports analogies.

Desires are not bad. You are not selfish; you are not greedy or indulgent. You are a being having a human experience, part of which is having desires. This is what motivates us to engage in life. There is a belief that desires are negative. Turns out it's contagious. Just in case you caught this sickness, stop it! Achieving our desires is our future and the life we design. Goals are the milestones we use to get there.

Finding your desires is a whole lot easier when you put them into this context. Because the fact is we do have desires we want to achieve. Look into your heart, your mind, your spirit. What do you want/desire so badly that an emotional response is provoked? A lot of times, you will find this is tied to your core values. One of my values is spiritual freedom. The freedom to break out of societal constraints, labels, and boxes, and live a life of bliss. That is my freedom. But to get there, I had to change my world.

Changing my world took time. It wasn't easy. My big-ticket goal to achieve this desire was my home. And I was specific. I worked with my husband to design exactly what we were looking for. Location, style, size, surroundings. All the things. Once we had our desire solid, I set the goals to get there. And to be honest, I manifested it too. In a few months, we found exactly the perfect house!

To make my point, I must tell you about this house. Give me just a moment to really show you the power of this. Desire: An East Coast Philadelphia 4-square, in the state of Washington (our kids live here), but in the desert, with 10-20 acres, trees, and amazing energy. This geographically is unrealistic. But I don't live in reality (insert evil laugh). I mentally create my reality.

And yes, we found exactly this. We live in a 1900's Philly 4-square in eastern Washington. There is nothing here! We see our neighbors 2 times a year, once in the winter when we are all digging out of 6' of snow and all the tractors and plows are running, and again in the spring when everyone discusses how farming will commence soon. There are no trees in sight outside of our property, which has beautiful, happy trees and loads of wildlife. We are in a desert/Mediterranean climate (yes, not all of Washington rains), and the house just loves us to bits. We love her too. Now how about that for setting a goal based on our desire and making it happen. It's impressive, when you think about it, the reality of this being possible.

Our desires can be grand and magnificent. Don't let your brain tell you it's not possible. Everything is possible! Again, look inside your heart, mind, and soul. What are your deep desires? Allow yourself to dream. Kinda like the ol' lottery question. "What will you do when you win the lottery?"

You just create the action through planning and goal setting. Goals provide structure, focus, and direction, enabling you to break through mental blocks and make progress towards your desire.

Firstly, think about what your desires are. Don't worry. At the end of this chapter, there is a space to write this down. Then, look at the achievable goals you need to have to create your action plan. Allowing you to have a clear destination in mind. It helps in defining what success looks like for you and provides a sense of purpose. By knowing exactly what you want to achieve, you can start taking the necessary steps to get closer to your desired outcomes.

Plus, setting achievable goals promotes a sense of motivation and empowerment. When goals are attainable, you are more inclined to believe in your ability to achieve them. This belief acts as a driving force, encouraging you to persist through challenges and obstacles. It instills a sense of confidence and self-efficacy, which is essential for overcoming mental blocks and developing a healthier mindset.

Developing an action plan of goals is important, as it outlines the specific steps and strategies needed to achieve your desires. An action plan provides a structured roadmap, breaking down the journey into manageable tasks and milestones. It helps you stay organized, focused, and on track.

Action plans enable you to anticipate potential obstacles and devise contingency plans. By considering potential challenges in advance, you can proactively prepare for them, reducing the likelihood of feeling overwhelmed or discouraged. This approach fosters resilience and adaptability, which are crucial for overcoming mental blocks and maintaining progress towards a healthier and happier lifestyle.

When you have a well-crafted action plan, it helps you stay accountable to yourself. Regularly reviewing and updating the plan allows you to monitor your progress and make any necessary adjustments. This process of self-reflection and self-correction promotes personal growth and development.

To illustrate the importance of identifying our desires and developing a comprehensive action plan, let's consider an example. Imagine someone is unhappy and hopeless about their physical fitness. Instead of simply wishing to become fit without any plan, they set a realistic goal of jogging for 10 minutes three times a week. They then develop an action plan that includes researching proper running techniques, scheduling specific jogging sessions in their calendar, and gradually increasing their jogging distance and intensity over time.

By following this structured approach, they were more likely to achieve their desire. They are less likely to become overwhelmed by the task at hand, as their action plan breaks it down into manageable goals. They can track their progress and celebrate small wins along the way, fostering a positive mindset and increased motivation.

This is all essential for overcoming mental blocks and moving towards a healthier and happier lifestyle. Providing direction, motivation, and accountability. By breaking down the journey into manageable goals, you can make progress, surpass mental hurdles, and achieve sustainable growth and fulfillment.

Now, let's take a look at the checklist I have created to help you implement these principles and start creating a healthier and happier lifestyle.

Checklist

1. **Define your desires:** Clearly identify what you want and why it is important to you. Don't skip the why! Set realistic and achievable goals that align with your values and desired outcomes.

2. **Break it down**: Break your desires into small goals, manageable tasks or milestones. This helps you to avoid feeling overwhelmed and allows for incremental progress.

3. **Develop a timeline:** Set deadlines or target dates for completing each task or milestone. This provides a sense of urgency and helps you stay focused and on track.

4. **Plan for challenges:** Anticipate potential obstacles or setbacks that may arise along the way. Consider alternative strategies or contingency plans to overcome challenges and keep moving forward.

5. **Gather information:** Do thorough research and gather relevant information to inform your decision-making process. Seek advice or input from experts or trusted individuals who can provide valuable insights.

6. **Evaluate options:** Consider different alternatives or approaches to achieving your goals. Evaluate the pros and cons of each option and determine which one aligns best with your needs and priorities.

7. **Assess resources:** Determine the resources (financial, time, skills, etc.) required to implement your action plan. Evaluate whether you have the necessary resources or if you need to seek additional support.

8. **Prioritize and organize:** Arrange tasks or steps in a logical order of priority. Establish a system to keep

track of your progress, such as a to-do list or project management tool.

9. **Take action:** Start implementing your action plan by taking the first step. Break inertia and overcome mental blocks by committing to action and embracing a growth mindset.

10. **Monitor and adjust:** Regularly review your progress and adjust your action plan as needed. Reflect on your achievements, learn from any mistakes or failures, and make necessary changes to stay on course.

11. **Celebrate milestones:** Acknowledge and celebrate your achievements on your journey. This fosters a positive mindset and increases motivation to keep going.

12. **Stay accountable:** Hold yourself accountable to your goals and action plan. Regularly assess your commitment and make necessary adjustments to ensure you are staying true to your vision and priorities.

By following this decision-making checklist, you can make informed choices, overcome mental blocks, and move closer to achieving a healthier and happier lifestyle.

Let's explore some examples that demonstrate how these principles can be applied in real-life situations.

Grace wanted to improve her relationships. Instead of setting unrealistic goals to completely eliminate negative relationships, she first identified why the relationships were this way. She then made the decisions necessary to improve all her relationships. Additionally, she worked on her perceptions and relationship programming. She was able to clearly see how she got where she was and where she wanted to be in her relationships. This specific goal gave her clarity on her desire and allowed her to take gradual steps toward achieving it.

Hannah desired to start a regular exercise routine but felt unmotivated and unsure of where to start. By setting an achievable goal of exercising for 20 minutes three times a week, she was able to build momentum and gradually increase her exercise duration. This sense of progress and achievement fostered motivation and encouraged her to continue her fitness journey.

Olivia struggled with procrastination and found it difficult to start tasks. By setting her intent to achieve her desire and developing an action plan with specific milestones, she was able to break down tasks into smaller, manageable goals.

Issy wanted to incorporate more self-care into her daily routine. Instead of overwhelming herself with numerous self-care activities, she set an achievable goal of practicing meditation for 10 minutes each morning. She then created an action plan that included finding a meditation app, setting a designated time and place for meditation, and gradually increasing the duration over time. This structured approach helped her establish a consistent self-care habit and improve her overall well-being.

These examples illustrate how setting achievable goals and creating action plans can provide direction, motivation, and organization, ultimately leading to progress and success in various aspects of life.

Now, these examples are what I would call stepping-stone desires. They would lead to bigger desires. Let's look at a case study of a big desire and the benefits of identifying the real desire and creating action plans in a real-life situation.

Case Study: Overcoming Mental Blocks When Achieving Desires and Action Plans

Taylor, a 35-year-old working professional, had been feeling unhappy and unmotivated in her life. She had been struggling to maintain consistent happiness and feeling overwhelmed by the idea that nothing consistently made her happy. Taylor's mental block was preventing her from taking the necessary steps towards improving.

Taylor faced several challenges that contributed to her mental block. She lacked a clear sense of direction and purpose, making it difficult for her to set specific goals. Additionally, she felt discouraged and lacked confidence in her ability to achieve her desire for happiness. Taylor needed a structured approach to break through her mental block and develop a healthier mindset.

Taylor worked with me to dig into identifying her desires and set achievable goals. This provided her with a clear destination and a sense of purpose without the overwhelm of doing it on your own.

Taylor developed a comprehensive action plan that included some discovery exercises to help us find what didn't work and what did. We then researched her reasons for them working or not. Making small adjustments and offering new alternatives to try, Taylor was able to start taking action and not be overwhelmed. This plan provided structure and direction for her journey.

By following her action plan, Taylor was able to build up her confidence and enjoyment in life. She went from struggling to do anything that made her happy, to finding several options that made her happy consistently.

She achieved small milestones and saw progress; she experienced a boost in her emotional well-being and felt a sense of accomplishment. Her mental well-being improved as she overcame her mental blocks.

Taylor encountered a few challenges along her happiness journey. Initially, she struggled with self-doubt and found it challenging to stay consistent with her discoveries.

Additionally, she experienced emotional discomfort and found it difficult to push through barriers.

Taylor learned the importance of believing in her ability to achieve her desires. As she developed confidence in her options, she became more resilient and motivated, enabling her to overcome mental blocks.

Throughout her happiness journey, Taylor realized the importance of adapting her action plan to address challenges and setbacks. This flexibility allowed her to maintain progress and avoid getting discouraged.

By setting achievable goals and developing a well-structured action plan, Taylor was able to overcome her mental blocks and make progress toward a joyful lifestyle. The clear goals provided her with direction and purpose, while the action plan helped her stay organized and focused. Through consistent effort and gradual progress, Taylor built resilience, gained confidence, and achieved sustainable growth and fulfillment.

This case study demonstrates the significance of goal setting and action planning in overcoming mental blocks and achieving personal growth. Taylor's journey emphasizes how breaking down larger ambiguous desires into smaller, manageable goals and tracking progress can pave the way for success. By fostering a belief in yourself, developing flexibility, and maintaining accountability, you can overcome mental hurdles and experience lasting positive change.

Now that we have examined Taylor's journey and the positive outcomes she achieved, identifying desires and action planning, let's take a look at some of the common mistakes to avoid when trying to overcome mental blocks and achieve personal growth.

A mistake most people make in this area is not properly identifying their desires. Many individuals tend to set goals that are not defined, which can lead to feelings of frustration and discouragement. To avoid this mistake, it is important to identify the why and setting specific, measurable, attainable, relevant, and time-bound (SMART goals). Additionally, individuals should consider their current circumstances, resources, and capabilities.

Another mistake people make is not developing a well-thought-out action plan. Without a plan, individuals may feel lost or overwhelmed, making it difficult to make progress toward their desires. To avoid this, it is important to create a detailed action plan that outlines the specific steps and strategies needed to achieve the desire. This plan should include milestones, a timeline, and potential solutions for anticipated obstacles.

To avoid common mistakes in this area, you should identify your desires and set achievable goals that align with your capabilities and circumstances. You should also develop a comprehensive action plan that outlines the necessary steps and strategies to reach each of your goals. By doing so, you can overcome mental blocks and create a truly purposeful life.

To ensure success in this area, it is crucial to address these mistakes and take the necessary steps to avoid them. With that being said, let's look at what we just covered. I don't want you to get lost.

Let's summarize this:

- **Identification:** Identify your real desires.
- **Define success:** Set achievable goals to define success and provide a sense of purpose.
- **Belief is your driving force:** Believe in your ability to achieve your desires and use that belief as a driving force.
- **Create a plan:** Develop a well-thought-out action plan to outline specific steps and strategies.
- **Plan for setbacks:** Anticipate obstacles and devise contingency plans to reduce overwhelm and maintain progress.

- **Stay accountable:** Regularly review and update your action plan to stay accountable and foster personal growth.

Dig in my friend.

1. What truly matters to me at the end of the day?

_____
_____
_____
_____

2. What are my long-term desires?

_____
_____
_____
_____

3. What potential obstacles or challenges do I need to overcome?

_____
_____
_____
_____

4. How will I hold myself accountable?

_____
_____
_____
_____

5. How will achieving these desires and goals support my personal growth and well-being?

_____
_____
_____
_____

6. How will I celebrate my wins?

_____
_____
_____
_____

But setting achievable goals and developing an action plan is just the beginning of our journey toward a healthier and happier lifestyle, allowing us to reach our true potential. In the next chapter, we will explore how you can incorporate simple yet profound spiritual practices into your daily routines, even amidst the chaotic hustle and bustle of our busy schedules. Keep reading to discover how these practices can bring deep inner peace and joy to your life.

Chapter 10

Spiritual Practices in a Busy World: Incorporating Sacred Rituals into Daily Life

"You don't have a soul. You are a soul. You have a body."

— **C.S. Lewis**

- Discover inner peace and purpose through daily spiritual practices.
- Find practical solutions to integrate spirituality into your busy schedule.
- Set the tone for your day with morning reflection and intention setting.
- Create rituals that bring stability and grounding to your spiritual journey.
- Connect with a supportive community and adapt your practices to fit your life.

If you haven't figured it out yet, this is the foundation of life. To reach your true potential, you must take control of your mind, body and spirit. Hence, this whole book has been designed around all my clients' experiences, along with my own. This works!

I'm going to go a little deeper into each of these areas we have discussed because I want you to understand how simple and easily adjusted they are to today's noisy world.

Incorporating spiritual practices into our daily routines can be a transformative experience, helping us find inner peace, purpose, and balance. Often, it may feel challenging to make time for spiritual practices amidst our busy schedules. However, with a thorough and supportive approach, we can find practical solutions to integrate spirituality seamlessly into our daily lives.

Begin by setting aside time each morning for reflection and intention setting. Whether it's through meditation, prayer, or quiet contemplation, this sacred time allows you to connect with your inner self and set the tone for the day ahead. During this time, you can focus on your values, goals, and mindset, fostering a sense of stability and purpose.

Start with any amount of time that works for you. Somedays, I do this for twenty minutes, while others, for two hours. It just depends on what is happening in my world.

When I'm manifesting a desire, I tend to do this for 2 hours. When I am having a normal day, and I just want to enrich others, well, it might be 30 minutes. I take the time to set my intention on my focus area. I check any goals I have around it and program my mind it will happen.

For example, say you just want to have a productive day. No distractions, just watching that to-do list shrink. You visualize what this looks like. Plan for what you will do if someone disrupts your productivity and believe it will happen. That's it, it's that simple.

Creating rituals provides a sense of structure and stability, grounding us in our life's journey. Choose activities that hold personal significance for you, such as lighting a candle, reciting mantras, affirmations, or reading. Engage in these rituals at specific times each day, reinforcing the stability they bring. Even simple acts like sipping a cup of tea or coffee with awareness and being present in the moment or taking a walk in nature can become powerful moments of our mind-body-spirit connection.

Each morning, I grab my water bottles, start the tea kettle and coffee pot, then head upstairs for my shower. I do my yoga, prayers, meditation, pattern digging, and set my intention for the day. I am filled with bliss, calm, and clarity, get more done by 9 a.m. than much of the population. This is how I like my rituals.

Just take a moment and think about how your morning or evening happened. What are the regular things you do? This is your ritual. Review it and see if it is helping you reach your true potential. If it's not, adjust it until it does.

Incorporate awareness into your daily routine to be present in every moment. Mindfulness can be practiced while performing routine tasks such as brushing your teeth, cooking, or even commuting. The key is to bring your full attention to the present moment, engaging all your senses. This practice cultivates a deep sense of connection with the world around you and elevates ordinary actions into experiences.

We have talked about the importance of surrounding ourselves with a supportive community. Where is this in your spiritual journey? Do you attend a church, circle, or temple? This can be done through joining local or online spiritual groups, attending workshops or retreats, or connecting with like-minded individuals on social media. You got options people; use them. Engaging with others who prioritize spirituality creates a stable and nurturing environment, reminding you of the importance of your personal journey and resources to continue your growth.

Remember that spirituality is not confined to specific practices or time commitments. It is a personal and flexible journey. If your schedule is particularly busy, find ways to adapt and simplify your spiritual practices. This may involve shortening your meditation sessions, incorporating moments during breaks at work, or finding spiritual meaning in everyday tasks. By adapting to our circumstances, we can maintain consistency and a sense of stability in our spiritual practices.

Incorporating these practices into our daily routines requires a deliberate and thoughtful approach. By setting aside time for reflection and intention setting, creating rituals, cultivating awareness, seeking support, and adapting to your circumstances, you can seamlessly integrate spirituality into your busy life. Remember, it is the quality of our intention and attention that matters most, rather than the quantity of time spent. By nurturing our spiritual well-being, we can create a stable and harmonious environment, fostering strength, passion, and abundance in our lives.

Now that we have explored the transformative power of incorporating spiritual practices into our daily routines, let's look at a checklist that can help us seamlessly integrate spirituality into our busy lives.

Checklist

1. **Reflect and Set Intentions:** Take a few minutes each morning for reflection and intention setting. Connect with your inner self and clarify your values, goals, and desired mindset for the day ahead.

2. **Create Rituals:** Establish rituals that hold personal significance, such as lighting a candle or reading sacred texts. Practice these rituals at specific times each day to provide structure and stability to your spiritual journey.

3. **Be Mindfully Aware:** Incorporate mindfulness into your daily routine by being fully present in each moment. Whether it's brushing your teeth or commuting, bring your full attention to the task at hand and engage all your senses.

4. **Seek Support:** Surround yourself with a supportive community that shares similar spiritual beliefs. Join local or online spiritual groups, attend workshops or retreats, and connect with like-minded individuals on social media. Being around others who prioritize spirituality provides a stable and nurturing environment.

5. **Adapt and Simplify:** Understand that spirituality is flexible and personal. Adapt and simplify your spiritual practices to fit your schedule and circumstances. This may involve shortening

meditation sessions or finding spiritual meaning in everyday tasks.

Remember, it is the quality of your intention and attention that matters most in your spiritual practices. By incorporating these steps into your life, you can seamlessly integrate spirituality and create a stable and harmonious environment.

Let me share a few examples of others who have done this already.

Mia begins her day by setting aside ten minutes for meditation and reflection. She sits in a quiet corner of her bedroom, closes her eyes, and focuses on her breath, allowing her mind to quiet and her body to relax. During this time, she sets intentions for the day, affirming her values of compassion, patience, and gratitude. This daily practice helps her cultivate inner peace and clarity, leading to a more centered and purposeful day.

Mackenzie incorporates rituals into her daily routine to deepen her spiritual connection. Every evening before bed, she lights a candle on her bedside table and takes a few moments to quiet her mind and offer gratitude for the day. She then recites mantras that align with her spiritual beliefs, reinforcing positive thoughts and intentions. This simple ritual brings a sense of stability and comfort, reminding Mackenzie of her connection to something greater than herself.

Maria practices mindful awareness throughout her day to stay present and connected. While cooking dinner for her family, she fully immerses herself in the process, noticing the colors, smells, and textures of the ingredients. She focuses on the simple act of chopping vegetables, savoring each moment without judgment or distraction. By doing so, she experiences a sense of peace, joy, and gratitude for the nourishment she is providing for her loved ones.

Dalia seeks support by joining a local spiritual group that meets weekly. She attends their gatherings, where they engage in discussions, guided meditations, and shared practices. Being part of this supportive community allows Dalia to connect with others who share her spiritual beliefs, providing encouragement and inspiration on her journey. Through these interactions, she feels a sense of belonging and finds strength and guidance in the collective wisdom of the group.

Lisa adapts and simplifies her spiritual practices to fit into her busy schedule. She often finds herself rushing in the mornings, so she starts her day by taking a few moments to connect with nature. As she walks from her car to her office, she breathes in the fresh air, feels the warmth of the sunlight on her skin, and notices the beauty of the trees and flowers around her. In these brief moments, Lisa finds a sense of grounding and connection, infusing her day with a touch of spirituality amidst her busy routine.

These examples demonstrate how individuals can incorporate spiritual practices into their daily lives, finding ways to create sacred moments and infuse their routines with spirituality. By making these practices a priority and adapting them to fit their lifestyles, individuals can experience transformative shifts and cultivate inner peace, purpose, and balance.

Now that we have explored some examples of how individuals can incorporate spiritual practices into their daily lives, we will take a closer look at a case study that showcases the transformative power of these practices. In this case study, we will examine how Victoria, a busy working professional, successfully integrates spirituality into her hectic schedule, resulting in increased well-being, clarity, and fulfillment.

Case Study: The Transformative Power of Daily Spiritual Practices

Victoria, a busy professional, always felt a longing for a deeper sense of purpose and inner peace. She often struggled to find time for spiritual practices amidst her demanding work schedule and family obligations. Determined to make a change, Victoria decided to incorporate spiritual practices into her daily routine to create a more balanced and fulfilled life.

Every morning, Victoria set aside 10 minutes for reflection and intention setting. She sat in a quiet corner of her home, closed her eyes, and practiced deep breathing. During this time, she reflected on her values, goals, and desired mindset for the day. Victoria also wrote down affirmations that aligned with her spiritual beliefs and intentions.

Victoria introduced rituals into her daily routine to bring a sense of structure and stability. Each evening, she lit a candle in her bedroom and spent a few minutes in silent prayer. Before going to bed, she read a few pages from a spiritual text that resonated with her. These rituals created a sacred space for Victoria to connect with her spirituality and set a peaceful tone for her evening.

Victoria started practicing mindfulness throughout her day. Instead of rushing through routine tasks, she made a conscious effort to be fully present in the moment. For example, while preparing breakfast, she focused on the aroma and taste of each ingredient, feeling a greater sense of gratitude and connection to the food she was about to consume. Victoria also practiced mindful breathing during her commute, using the time to center herself and find inner calm.

She joined an online spiritual community that aligned with her beliefs. She participated in virtual workshops and discussions, connecting with like-minded individuals who shared their spiritual insights and experiences. Victoria found a supportive environment where she could freely express her thoughts, ask questions, and receive guidance from others on their spiritual journey. This community became a source of inspiration and encouragement for Victoria to stay committed to her daily spiritual practices.

After several months of integrating spirituality into her daily routine, Victoria noticed significant positive changes. She reported feeling a greater sense of inner peace, purpose, and balance in her life. Victoria also experienced reduced stress levels and improved overall well-being. She found it easier to navigate challenges and setbacks with resilience and positivity. Additionally, Victoria's relationships with her family and colleagues improved as she approached them with a newfound sense of compassion and understanding.

Victoria encountered some challenges along her journey to incorporate daily spiritual practices into her routine. Initially, she struggled with consistency, often succumbing to her busy schedule and neglecting her spiritual commitment. Victoria also faced resistance from family and friends who did not understand or value the importance of spirituality in her life. However, with determination and support from her online community, she learned to overcome these obstacles and stay committed to her spiritual practices.

Victoria learned that integrating spirituality into a daily routine requires discipline, adaptability, and self-compassion. She realized that it is the quality of intention and attention she brings to her practices that matter most, rather than the quantity of time spent. Victoria also discovered that flexibility is key to sustaining her spiritual journey during busy periods. By adapting and simplifying her practices, she could maintain a sense of stability and spiritual connection even during demanding times.

Victoria's commitment to incorporating spiritual practices into her daily routine had a significant impact on her life. By staying strong and adhering to her routine, she experienced a profound transformation. Victoria found purpose, which permeated various aspects of her life. She learned to navigate challenges with resilience, fostered stronger relationships, and became a source of inspiration for others. Victoria's daily spiritual practices became a foundation for her overall well-being and contributed to her continued growth on her spiritual journey.

Victoria made a few mistakes during her journey. Heck, we all do. By learning from Victoria's experiences, we can navigate potential obstacles and ensure the successful integration of spirituality into our daily routines. I have a few more below so you can be sure to avoid them.

- Not making time for reflection and intention setting: Many people may feel too busy to set aside a few minutes each morning for reflection and intention setting. This can be avoided by recognizing the importance of this sacred time and prioritizing it as a necessary part of the daily routine.

- Neglecting to create rituals: Rituals provide structure and stability in our spiritual journey, yet many people may not create personal rituals that hold significance for them. To avoid this mistake, individuals should choose activities that are meaningful to them and engage in them consistently.

- Lacking mindful awareness: Mindfulness is key in spiritual practices, but often, people neglect to be present in every moment. This can be overcome by incorporating mindfulness into routine tasks and bringing full attention to the present moment.

- Not seeking support: Many individuals may try to navigate their spiritual journey alone, without the support of a community that shares similar beliefs. To avoid this, it is important to actively seek out and engage with supportive communities, both online and offline.

- Being inflexible in spiritual practices: Some people may confine spirituality to specific practices or time commitments, which can be challenging to maintain in a busy schedule. To avoid this, individuals should adapt and simplify their spiritual practices according to their circumstances, finding ways to incorporate spirituality into everyday tasks and making it a personal and flexible journey. And give yourself some grace. In the beginning, if you accidentally wake up late, or maybe you get sick. Don't force yourself to do it. You need to want to do it. And there is always tomorrow.

By avoiding these mistakes and following the suggestions provided, you can seamlessly integrate spirituality into your daily life, finding inner peace, purpose, and balance.

I hope you get the point of these and how simple they are to incorporate. Just follow what we covered below.

- **Peace and Purpose Daily:** Find inner peace and purpose by incorporating spiritual practices into your daily routine.
- **Reflect:** Set aside a few minutes each morning for reflection and intention-setting, connecting with your values and goals for the day ahead.
- **Create your rituals:** Create rituals that provide structure and stability, such as lighting a candle or reading sacred texts, to deepen your spiritual journey.
- **Practice makes perfect:** Practice mindful awareness in each moment, whether it's brushing your teeth or commuting, to cultivate a deeper connection with the world around you.

- **Identify Supportive people:** Seek support from a community that shares your spiritual beliefs, whether it's joining local groups or connecting online to nurture your personal journey.

One last time! Let's dig into this.

1. What is the first step you're going to take to incorporate spiritual practices into your daily routines?

_____
_____
_____
_____

2. What practice can you use to connect with your inner self?

_____
_____
_____
_____

3. What activities can become powerful moments of spiritual connection?

_____
_____
_____
_____

4. What communities have you identified that you can join to help support your spiritual journey?

_____
_____
_____
_____

5. What time of day are you going to intentionally practice?

_____
_____
_____
_____

CONCLUSION

I know it wasn't always easy, but YOU DID IT! You made it to the end of this book! Congratulations! This shows how determined you are to reach your true potential.

My last piece of advice. Don't let society suck you in. Beat to your own drum and manifest your possibilities, dreams, and desires. Fulfill Your Purpose! This is why we are here!

Hopefully, you noticed the patterns in these chapters and how everything ties together. Any repetition was intentional. Sometimes, we need to hear or read it repeatedly. Most of us are programmed to move quickly and focus on the end result. Reaching your potential isn't about the race. It's about the journey. You can take control of your mind, body, and soul, giving you the freedom to truly unlock your potential.

Can you see "Unlocking Your True Potential: Harnessing Control for a Blissful Body, Mind, and Soul" offers a comprehensive guide to empower you on your journey towards reclaiming your life. Was it what you thought this journey would be like?

Remember, you have the power to rewrite your story. Embrace the wisdom within these chapters, and review all the work you did on the pages. Watch as your life transforms into one of infinite possibilities. Get ready to unlock your true potential and witness the incredible journey that lies ahead!

You aren't alone. We are here for you. If you find yourself feeling unmotivated and scared to lose momentum, don't! If you are ready to take the next step and keep expanding your personal growth and potential, join us! Our program, "Mind Body Spirit Connection: Unlocking Your True Potential," was created specifically for you! We provide ongoing support through live classes, coaching, and community for you to grow and advance your personal journey.

It's all designed around you to help you unlock your true potential and create positive changes in your life. Our team of experienced coaches will guide you through the process of self-discovery and personal growth. We provide the necessary tools and resources to help you stay on track and reach your goals.

Our live classes, coaching, and community will give you the support you need to stay motivated and keep expanding your personal growth and potential. It's designed to help you achieve your desires and create positive changes in your life.

Take the next step and join us today. Unlock your true potential and create the life you've always wanted!

Sign up now and get started on your journey to success!

Visit www.unlockyourtruepotential.com for more information and to get started today!

I wish you great success on your journey in this life. Thank you for taking the time for you and really digging in. Growing and building hope and confidence for yourself. I admire anyone who takes this journey, and I know you can and will achieve your true potential.

Many blessings,

Jessica

MEET THE AUTHOR

Unlock Your True Potential: Find Happiness, Bliss, and Purpose with Jessica Martin – Certified Coach, Astrologer, Yoga and Meditation Instructor, Speaker, Healer, and Herbalist.

Embark on a transformational journey like no other, guided by the expert hand of Jessica Martin. With her extensive experience and qualifications, she is uniquely qualified to help you unlock your true potential and discover the happiness, bliss, and purpose you've been searching for in life.

Having helped thousands of students and clients since 2014, Jessica has mastered the art of empowering individuals to tap into their inner potential. As a highly respected coach and teacher in the field of spirituality and healing, she possesses a vast range of tools and techniques to cater to your individual needs and desires.

As you join Jessica on your personal journey, rest assured that you are being guided by someone who has walked the path herself. Jessica's transformative experiences have provided her with invaluable insights and wisdom, making her an ideal mentor to help you take back control of your life in a confident and purpose-driven way.

Now is the time to ignite the spark within you and step onto the clear path that leads to lasting joy and fulfillment. With Jessica's guidance, you will learn to cultivate self-awareness, embrace your unique strengths, and identify the passions that light you up from within. Her nurturing yet empowering approach will inspire you to take action and create the life you've always dreamed of.

Don't miss out on the opportunity to connect with Jessica and her transformative teachings. Through her engaging and conversational writing style, you will feel like you have a trusted friend cheering you on every step of the way.

Unlock your true potential and find happiness, bliss, and purpose with Jessica Martin – the guide and mentor who is here to help you reclaim your life and create the joyful existence you deserve. Together, you can embark on a journey toward personal growth and ultimate fulfillment. It's time to take that leap and embrace a life of happiness and purpose.

www.ingramcontent.com/pod-product-compliance
Lightning Source LLC
Chambersburg PA
CBHW030037100526
44590CB00011B/241